D1409229

Rocky Sung's Guide to Chinese Astrology and Feng Shui

The Year of the Snake

2001

Rocky Sung

Thorsons

Thorsons
An Imprint of HarperCollins*Publishers*
77–85 Fulham Palace Road
Hammersmith, London W6 8JB

The Thorsons website address is: www.thorsons.com

Published by Thorsons 2000

1 3 5 7 9 10 8 6 4 2

© Rocky Siu-Kwong Sung 2000

Rocky Siu-Kwong Sung asserts the moral right to
be identified as the author of this work

A catalogue record for this book
is available from the British Library

ISBN 0 00 710398 0

Printed in Great Britain by
Omnia Books Ltd, Glasgow

All rights reserved. No part of this publication may be
reproduced, stored in a retrieval system, or transmitted,
in any form or by any means, electronic, mechanical,
photocopying, recording or otherwise, without the prior
permission of the publishers.

Contents

Rocky Sung is a respected authority on Feng Shui, highly commendable for his honesty, directness and professionalism. He studies all factors involved and considers all available resources before making any recommendations. He does not propose major changes that will waste current resources, but rather suggests improvements that will maximize their full Feng Shui potential. His expertise and improvements have induced a more positive relationship between man and his environment.

Andre G. Rolli, General Manager,
Westin Hotel, Shanghai

About the Author

Sung Siu-Kwong, hereafter referred to as Rocky Sung, is instantly recognizable by the international Chinese community as the top Feng Shui Master of what must surely be the Feng Shui capital of the world – Hong Kong.

His many best-selling Chinese books on Feng Shui, a successful Feng Shui television programme viewed by Chinese communities across the globe, countless interviews on international television shows, such as on CNN, press and magazine interviews conducted in many languages, plus his reputation as a scrupulous results-driven consultant, have assured him this international recognition.

Born in China, Sung grew up in Hong Kong. He graduated from Taiwan University with a degree in history, and went on to obtains his Master's Degree from the University of Illinois. His interest in Feng Shui dates back to his schooldays, when his love of hiking found him out on the rigorous mountain trails of the territory. It was on these outdoor expeditions that an elderly Master taught him how to locate the 'veins of the dragon', or the flow of the mountain. As his knowledge of Chinese history grew, so too did his knowledge of this ancient Chinese tradition.

Sung has millions of followers and an enviable multinational blue-chip client list that includes the prestigious retail chain Marks

& Spencer, the Swire Group of Companies and the Westin International Hotel Group.

Westerners in Hong Kong have long followed the beliefs of their Chinese counterparts; now, as the entire Western world expresses an interest in Eastern philosophies and traditions, the name Rocky Sung has become increasingly synonymous with the art of Feng Shui throughout the world.

He has offices in Hong Kong and Los Angeles, and family contacts in New York.

Introduction

This book is unique and outstanding because it consists of the following four key factors that distinguish it from all the other books about Chinese Horoscope:

1 The application of the traditional Stars in the Chinese Horoscope into the calculation of the fate of different Signs.
2 The use of proverbs to indicate the fate of a Sign for a particular month.
3 The application of Feng Shui to improve the fortune of different Signs.
4 An easy-to-read chart to remind readers of how to 'do the right things at the right time every day' in 2001 (the Day-by-day Analysis of Luck).

Application of Traditional Stars of the Chinese Horoscope

This is the first book in English which uses a pure Chinese Horoscope methodology to predict the future. It is not at all influenced by Western Astrology. Chinese traditional Astrology is completely different to Western Astrology.

The Chinese method of predicting the future was developed

some 2,000 years ago, and calculated according to the distribution of Stars within a specific Sign. The number of Lucky and Unlucky Stars within a Sign determines a person's fate for the year. The distribution varies on a year-to year basis for each Sign, therefore the fate of each Sign changes annually.

This calculating system has been practiced in China for centuries and has proved to be quite effective. I have applied this system in the writing of my Chinese-language yearly fortune book, which has sold in large numbers since 1985.

The Lucky and Unlucky Stars of the Chinese Horoscope have a very long history. Given the history of Chinese predictions without applying the traditional method, as is so often seen in Western books on Chinese Astrology, is definitely incorrect. Unfortunately a lot of so-called 'Chinese Horoscope' books in print are therefore inaccurate.

I have no bias against Western or Indian Astrology – quite the contrary, I have a deep and sincere respect for them. However, a mixture of Chinese and Western Astrology diminishes the substance and destroy the basic nature of both.

Considering that most non-Chinese readers have no knowledge of the Stars that influence the Chinese Astrological predictions, I have explained the origins, meaning and modern implication of each one. After reading the Stars, both Lucky and Unlucky, which apply to your Sign for the forthcoming year, you will have a clear picture of your fate.

This book provides the reader with predictions for the entire year, with daily reference charts for every day of the year in the Chinese Calendar (see pages 210 – 313).

The monthly prognosis is to prepare the reader on how to face each month. It will give you the opportunity to protect yourself when facing bad luck, and it will give you the opportunity to activate initiatives when you know you are heading for good luck.

The 12 Chinese Horoscope Signs

The Snake
The Horse
The Sheep (Goat)
The Monkey
The Rooster
The Dog
The Pig
The Mouse (Rat)
The Ox
The Tiger
The Rabbit
The Dragon

Individuals are classified according to their birth date. The chart on page xiii will allow readers to check which is their Sign.

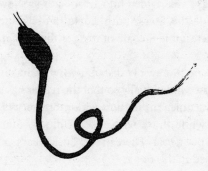

Snake	Horse	Sheep	Monkey
Dragon			Rooster
Rabbit			Dog
Tiger	Ox	Mouse	Pig

The 12 Signs are divided into 12 squares as shown above. The distribution of the Stars, both Lucky and Unlucky, with the squares will determine the fate of each of the 12 Signs for the year ahead.

The Stars are not evenly distributed; this makes a difference. Each Star is listed individually so that the reader has a clear picture of his or her fortune. Those Signs with more Lucky Stars will have a good year, while those with more Unlucky Stars will have a rough, even a poor, year. There are 20 Lucky Stars and 46 Unlucky Stars mentioned in this book.

Proverbs and Fortune

Each chapter for a particular Sign has a General Overview of the Year for 2001, followed by Monthly In-depth Forecasts. Each of these monthly sections begins with a proverb, to enable readers to know at a glance precisely what challenges they are going to face in a given month.

Proverbs are derived from the experiences of daily life. Therefore, after very careful consideration I have decided upon an appropriate proverb to summarize the monthly fortune for each Sign. Through this I hope that readers will have a much better understanding of their fortune for each month.

I sincerely hope that this method of my own will benefit readers throughout the world.

Using Feng Shui

The main Feng Shui tactics are discussed at the end of the monthly forecasts of each sign, as a suggestion to improve fortune practically and effectively. Each outlines the Feng Shui directions, colours, lucky numbers and lucky charms for each Sign.

These Feng Shui tactics are practical and effective in improving the fortune of every sign. They are based on combining the calculation of the Five Elements, the Yin and Yang, and the distribution of Lucky and Unlucky Stars throughout the year.

Just as different kinds of medicine will suit different people, different Feng Shui tactics will suit different Signs. To avoid taking the wrong 'medicine', readers should not try to apply the Feng Shui recommended for any Sign but their own.

Day-by-day Analysis of Luck

From the experiences of their daily lives through numerous generations, the ancient Chinese found that certain activities would meet with much greater success if undertaken on certain days. Along the same line, certain things can go wrong if attempted on the wrong day. Thus the ancient Chinese realized that there was a close correlation between human activities and certain days. Consequently, the concept of 'doing the right thing at the right time every day' has been deeply ingrained into the Chinese psyche and society for centuries.

The Day-by-day Analysis of Luck tables will prove helpful in improving one's overall fortune. The same charts have appeared in my Chinese-language books, and have proven useful to my readers over the past 15 years.

The charts begin at 1 January 2001 and end at 31 December 2001. Beneath the charts there are brief forecasts for the Signs, to help readers know what they are going to face during that particular period of time. This is meant as a helpful supplement to the Monthly In-depth Forecasts for the Signs in the previous chapters.

According to the Chinese calendar commonly used, the year of Snake begins on 4 January 2001 and ends on 11 February 2002 of the Western calendar. But the Chinese traditional astrology has different ideas about the division of the year. The 'Lap Chung Day' 立春日 – that is, the 'Day of the Beginning of Spring', is used as a division line of the year. Consequently, the year of Snake begins on 4 February 2001 and ends on 3 February 2002 according to traditional Chinese astrology. As a writer of fortune books for more than 15 years, I am sure that the calculation of fate for the 12 signs within the year is made more accurate by using this traditional system.

How to Establish Your Chinese Sign

1905 – Snake	1906 – Horse **	1907 – Sheep **	1908 – Monkey **
1909 –Rooster	1910 – Dog **	1911 – Pig **	1912 – Mouse **
1913 – Ox	1914 – Tiger	1915 – Rabbit **	1916 – Dragon **
1917 – Snake	1918 – Horse	1919 – Sheep **	1920 – Monkey **
1921 – Rooster	1922 – Dog	1923 – Pig **	1924 – Mouse **
1925 – Ox	1926 – Tiger	1927 – Rabbit **	1928 – Dragon **
1929 – Snake	1930 – Horse	1931 – Sheep **	1932 – Monkey **
1933 – Rooster	1934 – Dog	1935 – Pig **	1936 – Mouse **
1937 – Ox	1938 – Tiger	1939 – Rabbit **	1940 – Dragon **
1941 – Snake	1942 – Horse	1943 – Sheep **	1944 – Monkey **
1945 – Rooster	1946 – Dog	1947 – Pig	1948 – Mouse **
1949 – Ox	1950 – Tiger	1951 – Rabbit	1952 – Dragon **
1953 – Snake	1954 – Horse	1955 – Sheep	1956 – Monkey **
1957 – Rooster	1958 – Dog	1959 – Pig	1960 – Mouse **
1961 – Ox	1962 – Tiger	1963 – Rabbit	1964 – Dragon **
1965 – Snake	1966 – Horse	1967 – Sheep	1968 – Monkey **
1969 – Rooster	1970 – Dog	1971 – Pig	1972 – Mouse **
1973 – Ox	1974 – Tiger	1975 – Rabbit	1976 – Dragon **
1977 – Snake	1978 – Horse	1979 – Sheep	1980 – Monkey **
1981 – Rooster	1982 – Dog	1983 – Pig	1984 – Mouse
1985 – Ox	1986 – Tiger	1987 – Rabbit	1988 – Dragon
1989 – Snake	1990 – Horse	1991 – Sheep	1992 – Monkey
1993 – Rooster	1994 – Dog	1995 – Pig	1996 – Mouse
1997 – Ox	1998 – Tiger	1999 – Rabbit	2000 – Dragon
2001 – Snake	2002 – Horse	2003 – Sheep	2004 – Monkey

According to the Chinese Horoscope, people are classified into a certain Sign according to their birth year. This chart will help you to establish your exact Sign. Please refer to the first page of each Sign for more detailed information.

There is a difference in year division between the Chinese Calendar and the Western Calendar. 4 February of the Western Calendar is the dividing line. For example, if a person was born on 3 February 1998, then he is considered to be an Ox. But if he was born on 5 February 1998, then he is considered to be a Tiger.

Occasionally this dividing line changes to 5 February. This will mean a slight adjustment. These exceptional years are indicated on this chart by **.

Chapter One

The

Snake

Years of the Snake

1917 (4/Feb/17—3/Feb/18)	1965 (4/Feb/65—3/Feb/66)
1929 (4/Feb/29—3/Feb/30)	1977 (4/Feb/77—3/Feb/78)
1941 (4/Feb/41—3/Feb/42)	1989 (4/Feb/89—3/Feb/90)
1953 (4/Feb/53—3/Feb/54)	2001 (4/Feb/01—3/Feb/02)

Distribution of the Stars within the Sign for 2001

Lucky Stars	Unlucky Stars
Heavenly Salvation	Floating Up and Down
God of Salvation	Bloody Knife
The Eight Chiefs	Lying Corpse
	Sword's Edge
	Watch-dog of the Year
	Earthly Threat
	Pointing at the Back

Lucky Stars

Heavenly Salvation

'Heavenly Salvation' is one of the three Salvation Stars, which assist people in getting out of problems and disasters. Its appearance is a good omen.

When this Star appears, people have to stick to what they believe in and not give up, even if the situation appears impossible. When most needed they will get crucial assistance leading to a breakthrough.

God of Salvation

Ancient Chinese peasants often led a precarious existence, vulnerable as they were to threats such as wars, floods, droughts and famines. However, they believed that in critical times the God of Salvation would protect them from total destruction.

There are three 'Salvation' Stars in the Chinese Horoscope, of which this is considered to be the most powerful. It is generally regarded as having the power to suppress negative influences from any Unlucky Stars within the same Sign.

The Eight Chiefs

In the traditional Chinese ruling hierarchy, eight chiefs helped the emperor to govern the whole country. Although theoretically under the three prime ministers, they nonetheless had enough authority to keep everything in order.

When this Star appears, people will be promoted, and possess the power to rule and to scare off any challengers.

Unlucky Stars

Floating Up and Down

The Chinese have always suffered from the periodic flooding of the Yellow River, the so-called 'Sorrow of China'. They know from experience how dangerous it is to be caught and be floating up and down in the surging current of a flooding river.

Similarly, when this Star appears, people need to stay alert during this rough year so that they won't be carried away by the swift currents, or even drowned.

Bloody Knife

Knives, and other deadly weapons, were not commonly welcomed by the ancient Chinese, who preferred to live in peace. Similarly, a bloody knife was definitely a very bad omen associated with violence and killing.

When this Star appears, it is important to maintain one's temper, and avoid quarrels and fights, which will only bring unpleasant consequences.

Lying Corpse

In ancient China, to die peacefully at home was considered to be a blessing. In contrast, to die in an accident in the street or some other public place was considered the worst thing that could happen. Such unexpected and 'poorly timed' deaths were considered to be a kind of divine retribution for a person's bad deeds.

When this Star appears, be very careful not to commit any wrong-doings, and at the same time pay special attention to safety when engaged in outdoor activities.

Sword's Edge

Swords, as well as knives were not favoured by the peace-loving ancient Chinese. People would easily be hurt by the sharp edges of these dangerous weapons.

Consequently, the 'Sword's Edge' Star is considered to be a bad omen, calling for precautionary measures regarding your personal safety. This is especially relevant when engaging in outdoor activities and handling sharp objects.

Watch-dog of the Year

In Chinese mythology, a very fierce animal called 'Year' went about swallowing people just as a New Year was ushered in. To protect themselves the ancient Chinese used firecrackers to scare it away. Over time, this fierce animal would be tamed and became the Watch-dog of the Year among the Chinese folk. Still, it could be quite dangerous if irritated.

When this Star appears, it is best to behave, keep a low profile and take care not to offend anyone. To avoid problems, keep in mind the phrase 'let sleeping dogs lie.'

Earthly Threat

The ancient Chinese believed that malevolent spirits brought dangers and problems into their daily lives. Of these, 'Earthly Threat' was considered to be the least dangerous and damaging of the four 'Threats' in the Chinese horoscope.

When this Star appears, people should be extra careful about road safety.

Pointing at the Back

Based on their long struggle for survival, the ancient Chinese realized that the most dangerous enemies were those behind one's back. Such people lay in wait for an opportunity to attack, either verbally or physically, without warning.

When this Star appears, people need to hide their weaknesses and be aware of any hidden enemies or gossip around them.

General Overview of the Year

This year will be a very good time for the Snake to concentrate on new developments in business and investments. Snakes will get satisfactory rewards at year end if they can keep on going without too many interruptions. Distraction and lack of discipline will be the two major setbacks this year. Most important of all, Snakes should try to protect themselves from being attacked from behind by the hidden enemies around them.

Financially this will be a fortunate year for Snakes, and they will receive satisfactory incomes from different sources.

Snakes will have nothing to worry about regarding their health, but they should take extreme care when it comes to road safety.

Unfortunately, Snakes won't have too much luck in love affairs this year.

Career	***
Money	****
Health	***
Love	*

**** = Very Fortunate/*** = Pretty Good/* = Unsatisfactory

Career ***

Distraction and lack of discipline will be the two major setbacks to overcome this year, so that Snakes must try their best to avoid these two pitfalls. They will see splendid achievements if they can concentrate more on their new projects and investments. The Snake will have better luck at work during the second, third, seventh, eighth and the last month of the year. Snakes should try to make good use of these five months if they want to be more successful this year.

Snakes should try to reach out a helping hand to people who really need help; by doing so they will benefit themselves as well. One thing Snakes have to keep in mind throughout the year is that they should try to settle disputes as soon as possible and never let them get out of control. Although Snakes will face different challenges throughout the year, they will have the necessary support from subordinates and partners whenever needed. Most important of all, they will have enough guts and power to scare off any challengers.

Money ****

This will be a fortunate year for the Snake in money matters. Snakes will enjoy satisfactory incomes from different sources. However, they should never try their luck in gambling especially during the third, fourth, tenth and eleventh month. Should they be tempted they will lose a lot of money – probably much more than they ever anticipated. On the other hand, Snakes will have better luck with money during the second, eighth and the last month of the year.

Health ***

Snakes will be quite healthy this year, yet they must watch out for their road safety carefully. They must walk and drive with extreme care, particularly during the third and sixth month. Apart from this, Snakes must try to protect themselves from being hurt by sharp knives, razors and so on during the ninth month. It would be much better for Snakes to take short breaks or holidays to refresh themselves from time to time throughout the year. However, they have to pay attention to hygiene (such as the cleanliness of their food) when they are away from home.

Love *

Although Snakes are quite keen to get better acquainted with potential love interests, unfortunately they won't have too much luck in this area over the year. They should try to take it easy and never be too aggressive in love affairs this year. However, they will have better luck during the sixth, seventh, eighth and the last month of the year.

According to traditional Chinese astrology, the distributions of the Lucky and Unlucky Stars within a Sign will more or less determine a person's fate in a particular year. Just as the distributions of the Stars change from year to year, however, they also change from month to month. Each Sign's fate for the year and for each month is calculated according to this basic rule.

Monthly In-depth Forecasts
The First Month (4 February – 4 March)

Know thyself

The fortune of the Snake will fluctuate from time to time throughout the month, so it wouldn't be wise to start any new projects or new investments at this stage. However, it is the time for Snakes to re-evaluate their business and themselves objectively. The more they know about their weak and strong points, the more successful they will be in their future developments. Otherwise, their careers and their personal life will suffer eventually. Besides this, Snakes should try to keep a low profile in order to avoid attacks from the jealous people around them.

Snakes will have some luck in lottery and gambling. Having said this, they will find that their expenses will be greater than their income right now. This won't be a profitable month for Snakes, so it will be much better for them to wait for another time to make investments.

Although Snakes are anxious to get acquainted with a possible new loved one this month, they won't have too much luck in this matter right now.

The Second Month (5 March – 4 April)

Faith is the first requisite in success

Snakes will be quite creative and productive at work this month, so they should try to make good use of this time if they wish to have a successful year. However, they should try to concentrate on a major project only rather than fooling around with several minor ones. Faith and enthusiasm will be the two important factors in their success. Otherwise, all their efforts will be in vain. If Snakes are able to win the faith and confidence of their subordinates and clients, their success will be multiplied in the near future.

This is one of the Snake's most fortunate months for money affairs. There will be a small amount of unexpected income at the end of the month. If someone invites them into a joint venture in investments it will be well worth thinking about.

Any unreasonable suspicion will seriously hurt a love relationship during this period. Snakes should try to have faith and mutual understanding with their lovers, or they will face a broken relation.

The Third Month (5 April – 4 May)

Unity is strength

This is one of the most favourable months of the year for Snakes because of the appearance of several Lucky Stars within the Sign. It will be quite possible for them to overcome most of the difficulties they face. However, they'll have a much better chance of success if they can forge a union with people involved in the same trade during this period. This united strength will prove to be very helpful for future business development. In any case, Snakes must try to keep control over this union.

Snakes will be quite healthy this month. All they have to worry about is their personal safety. They should pay particular attention to road safety.

Snakes will see satisfactory incomes from different sources this month. Unfortunately, their luck will drop to the bottom at the end of the month. Snakes must try to watch out for money traps or they will lose a lot of money. Snakes will have much better luck in money matters later in the year.

The Fourth Month (5 May – 4 June)

It is easier to pull down than to build up

Different kinds of difficulties and personal disputes will arise during this period, so that Snakes will have to put more time and effort in to settle them down as soon as possible. There will probably be a sudden drop in sales or production. Snakes should not ignore this. If they do, all their previous efforts will have been in vain. Just as the old saying says, 'It is easier to pull down than to build up.'

Snakes might suffer from a sudden collapse in the near future. However, a good business relationship can help them overcome adversity. Snakes should try not to be late nor too stubborn in business meetings, or the situation will become even worse.

This is definitely not a fortunate month in money matters for Snakes. They will turn out to be big losers if they try their luck in gambling and high-risk investments. In addition, Snakes should try not to show off too much, or they may become the victims of a robbery or even a kidnapping. It would be much better for Snakes to give up their extravagant habits and save more money for themselves.

Snakes should try not to be too aggressive in their love affairs or they will just scare their lovers away from them. Instead, they should try to take things easy. They may meet with a pleasant surprise by doing so.

The Fifth Month (5 June – 6 July)

Be patient and endure

This is one of the most unfavourable months of the year for Snakes. They will continue to be bothered by numerous difficulties and disputes, as they were last month, and will have to handle them patiently. The situation will get out of control if the Snake loses patience. It would be much better to seek professional advice about business troubles whenever needed. The major concern for Snakes during this period is not how to expand, but how to survive. Snakes must keep themselves calm, even though somebody may be deliberately trying to provoke them.

Snakes have to be very conservative in handling their money matters. It's very important for them to check if there are any loopholes in their financial systems. Unless they can do some repair work, they will suffer from a money problem eventually.

Care and patience will be the most efficient remedies for improving endangered love relationships.

The Sixth Month (7 July – 6 August)

Where there's a will, there's a way

Snakes should never give up at this time even though they may suffer under the burden of a heavy workload, because their situation will be much improved in the following months. Their major concern at this stage is try to build up their own determination and confidence at work. Just as the old saying goes, 'Where there's a will, there's a way,' Snakes must keep their will strong enough against any difficulties. Besides this, Snakes should try to concentrate more on the task at hand; distractions will only bring disappointments and failure.

Snakes might be discouraged by their previous failures in love affairs. However, they may meet with a good surprise if they would like to try their luck again this month. It's worthwhile to do so, since there will be nothing for them to lose.

Snakes will be somewhat exhausted from their heavy workloads this month, so they should try to look after their health. Besides this, they must mind their personal safety during outdoor activities. It's better to be safe than sorry.

The Seventh Month (7 August – 6 September)

A gambler is known by his chips

The Snake's fortune will be much improved this month, so it would be a suitable time to think about or to take action regarding future developments. Since the bargaining power of Snakes will become quite strong this month, they should try to sell their ideas to prospective clients or superiors. They are going to have a splendid future if they succeed in doing so. However, Snakes should not forget to show their ability at the same time. Just as the old saying says, 'Actions speak louder than words.' Snakes should try not to handle their business with empty words.

It's time for Snakes to improve their relationships with their lovers. A bouquet of beautiful flowers, an affectionate love letter or a romantic dinner will bring them a very nice surprise and an unforgettable memory.

Although this is one of the most fortunate months in money matters for Snakes, yet they have to watch their expenses carefully. They should take care of their money just as the gambler takes care of his chips. Snakes have to make sure that they will have enough chips on hand to last throughout the year.

The Eighth Month (7 September – 7 October)

A bird in the hand is worth two in the bush

Although this is another favourable month for Snakes, they should try not to be too ambitious, lest they suffer a sudden fall. Greediness and over-ambition will blind them to the road to success, and will be quite dangerous. 'A bird in the hand is worth two in the bush' – Snakes should keep this old saying in mind. Otherwise they may end up with no birds at all. In other words, Snakes must concentrate on their major tasks only, and not start any new projects until they have finished the old ones.

Snakes should try not to be too greedy in money matters during this period. If they try their luck in many different investments, they will be deeply disappointed by poor returns. However, they will have luck in lottery and gambling.

There will be a few attractive people running around Snakes, but they should not indulge themselves in sex and pleasure too much, or they will end up being very sorry. They should try to be faithful to their lovers and never cheat on them during this period of time.

The Ninth Month (8 October – 6 November)

Many hands make light work

Snakes will be quite capable at handling their business right now, but there will be numerous disputes and rumours flying about this month. They have to settle these as soon as possible or the situation will get out of control in the months to come. Snakes will be quite popular among their subordinates during this period, so they will have the necessary support from them whenever needed. Just as the old saying says, 'Many hands make light work.' Snakes will be able to carry out their projects without too much difficulties. Their major concern this month is to watch out for those jealous people around them. They should try to keep away from them instead of trying to confront them face to face.

Snakes must watch out for their personal safety and try to protect themselves against injuries from sharp knives and saws. This month is not a good time for a vacation. Snakes must mind the cleanliness of their food on trips if they have to take any during this period.

Snakes should try their best to avoid a serious quarrel with their lovers. They had better walk away for a while if they find their anger and emotions are out of control. Snakes will be quite busy in different social gatherings, and they have to take care to resist the temptation to gossip.

The Tenth Month (7 November – 6 December)

It never rains but it pours

Snakes have to keep themselves alert because this is the most unfavourable month for them within the year. Difficulties and problems will come one after another, so that Snakes must try to equip themselves psychologically to be prepared for the unexpected. The damage will be minimized if they keep their eyes wide open to watch out for possible danger. One thing Snakes have to keep in mind is that they can't afford to relax, because the dangers will keep on coming. Besides this, Snakes have to keep an eye on discipline among those people who work for them. If they don't, lack of discipline will become their major problem in the coming months. They should do something about this now.

This month is definitely not a fortunate month for Snakes in money matters. Snakes will probably suffer from money problems if they failed to keep to a tight budget in previous months.

Family will become a good shelter for Snakes this month. They will enjoy a sweet family life and forget about the heavy pressures from their work and money problems temporarily. Consequently, Snakes should try to show their care and affection to family members in return.

The Eleventh Month (7 December – 4 January)

Half a loaf is better than none

Fortunately, the Snake will be able to get out of the troubles of last month, yet they still have to be cautious in handling their business and money matters. They can't afford to make a serious mistake during this period. Therefore, Snakes have to double-check all their important documents, contracts and bills throughout the month. They should try to be satisfied with the things already in their hands, because half a loaf really is better than none during this period of time. Their contentment with their lot will keep them out of a lot of trouble and disputes that will be far beyond their control. Besides this, Snakes should try to give the necessary assistance to those people around them who need help. They are not only helping others, but helping themselves too by doing so.

Because the fortune of Snakes in money matters will fluctuate from time to time throughout the month, they should try to avoid gambling their money in high-risk investments or they will be in big trouble. They should never get involved in any loans or debts this month.

Snakes will be quite weak both physically and mentally during this period. They should try to keep away from unhygienic food and crowded places in order to protect themselves from infection.

The Twelfth Month (5 January – 3 February)

The new broom sweeps clean

Snakes will be quite creative and capable at work this month. There will be some major changes in their careers, and Snakes should not have too much trouble coping with these changes if they really care about their work. On the other hand, they will be left far behind if they refuse to do so. Concentration and discipline will be the two most important factors in the Snake's future success. Most important of all, Snakes will be able to reach an important agreement or sign a very important contract with major clients during this period. However, they have to try their best to keep it a secret before everything is all wrapped up.

Snakes will have a very good chance to find a new lover for themselves this month. They are turning to a new page in their love affairs. They shouldn't take it for granted, or this romance will only be a very short one.

The fortune of Snakes in money matters will be much improved during this period. They will have incomes from different sources. Yet they should try not to ask for a loan this month, or it will become a nightmare to them in the near future.

Using Feng Shui to Improve Fortune: Directions, Colours, Numbers and Lucky Charm

The ancient Chinese used the traditional Horoscope to predict their fortune on a yearly basis – and they used the art of Feng Shui to improve their luck.

It was their belief that the application of tactical Feng Shui would change their bad luck into good, and make their good luck improve even more.

This same method is still effective in today's modern world.

There are four main elements which I will use in tactical Feng Shui:

◆ Lucky Directions
◆ Lucky Colours
◆ Lucky Numbers
◆ Lucky Charm

This year will be a very good time for Snakes to concentrate on new developments in business and investments. They will gain satisfactory rewards at year-end if they keep on concentrating without too many interruptions. Snakes will have steady incomes from different sources. They will be quite healthy this year, but they should watch out closely for their road safety. Snakes should not be too aggressive in love affairs or they will scare their lovers away.

I would suggest applying the following Feng Shui tactics to improve luck so that Snakes don't have to worry too much about their fate within the year.

Lucky Directions

The most favourable directions of the year for the Snake are **Southeast, Southwest** and **Northeast**. Snakes should sleep or sit in these directions if they wish to improve their fortune.

To make this procedure very simple, divide the house or room into nine imaginary squares. Then, using a compass, check the exact direction of each square as shown in Figure 1. This will help to ensure that you do not make a mistake with the direction.

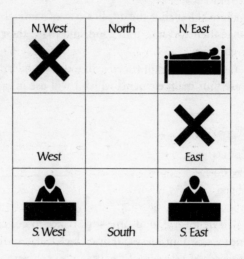

Figure 1

The Snake should sit in the relevant directions at work or while studying; this will ensure that achievements are much greater than the Stars intended. To improve health and achieve a good night's sleep, position your bed in the favourable direction shown (Northeast).

However, the Snake should try to keep away from the unfavourable directions of the year; that is, East and Northwest as shown in Figure 1. The Snake should try not to sit, work or sleep in these directions, so as to get rid of the negative influences lurking there.

Lucky Colours

According to Chinese tradition, each of the five Elements has its own representative colours. Fire is represented by red, pink and purple, Earth by yellow and brown, and so on. As a Feng Shui Master I would suggest **yellow**, **brown** and **white** as the Snake's lucky colours for the year 2001.

Use these colours in paints, wall coverings, rugs, drapes and curtains. This will be sure to bring good fortune throughout the year.

However, the Snake should try not to use green, red, pink or purple in 2001, to avoid bad luck.

Lucky Numbers

The lucky numbers for the Snake in 2001 are: **3** and **7**.

The Snake's fortune will be much improved by using these lucky numbers whenever possible. For example, if the Snake has a choice, the phone number 267-3773 is better than 268-4221 – because the former contains more threes and sevens, the Snake's two lucky numbers for the year.

Lucky Charm

Feng Shui Masters believe that special objects can be used as a medium between human beings and nature. The fortune of the recipient is greatly improved as the positive wave of energy from nature is passed through the object or 'lucky charm' on to the recipient.

The lucky charm for the Snake in 2001 is a pair of lions made of light yellow stone. This pair of lions stepping on stones with four Chinese characters, 'Spring', 'Summer', 'Autumn' and 'Winter', and a snake inscribed on them is shown below. For the best result, they should be placed in the southeast or the southwest direction of the house.

Chapter Two

The

Horse

Years of the Horse

1906 (5/Feb/06—4/Feb/07)   1954 (4/Feb/54—3/Feb/55)
1918 (4/Feb/18—4/Feb/19)   1966 (4/Feb/66—3/Feb/67)
1930 (4/Feb/30—4/Feb/31)   1978 (4/Feb/78—3/Feb/79)
1942 (4/Feb/42—4/Feb/43)   1990 (4/Feb/90—3/Feb/91)

Distribution of the Stars within the Sign for 2001

Lucky Stars	Unlucky Stars
The Sun	Yearly Threat
	Pool of Indulgence
	Black Cloud

Lucky Star

The Sun

The concept of Yin (female) and Yang (male) was essential in ancient Chinese culture. The Sun, representing energy and authority, is considered to be the most influential and important Yang symbol, similar to the god Apollo in Greek mythology.

When this Star appears in your Horoscope, evil things diminish just like snow melting under the warm sun.

Unlucky Stars

Yearly Threat

The ancient Chinese believed that malevolent spirits brought dangers and problems into their daily lives. The Star 'Yearly Threat' was one of these. Its appearance is a bad omen.

When this Star appears, people need to improve relations with others, especially with lovers and spouses, to avoid endless arguments and quarrels.

Pool of Indulgence

One of China's most cruel and wicked emperors, Emperor Zhou of the Shang Dynasty, built a pool which he filled with wine inside his luxurious palace. He invited his royal followers and beautiful women to come and be merry by drinking or even swimming in the wine. This symbol of over-indulgence warns against bad habits and self-indulgent behaviour.

If this Star appears within the Sign, people need to avoid bad habits – if they don't, they will miss out on good opportunities and waste a great deal of money.

Black Cloud

Just as black clouds gather before a heavy rainstorm, unseen black clouds, the ancient Chinese believed, gathered just before the outbreak of disaster. Chinese fortune-tellers would look for these 'black clouds' in face- or palm-reading. When they appeared, it was said life would become less clear, and people would easily lose their way.

The appearance of this Star means that people must maintain a keen perspective on what is happening, or they will not be able to find their way out of disputes. During this period it is important to save money and energy for unexpected 'thunderstorms'.

General Overview of the Year

Horses have to struggle very hard if they want to see any break-throughs in their business and studies this year. There will be numerous challenges and troubles ahead. However, Horses will have enough energy and authority to suppress almost all of these problems if they refuse to give up. Putting more time and effort in their careers and studies will not be good enough for Horses. They should also try to cut out their bad habits at the same time.

Financially this will not be a fortunate year for Horses, so they must try to be more conservative in handling their money. Although Horses will be in a pretty good shape physically and mentally, they must not indulge too much in sex and alcohol.

This will be a romantic year for Horses and they will be busily engaged in different kinds of social activities, but they must mind their words and behaviour carefully during these occasions.

Career *
Money **
Health ***
Love ****

**** = Very Fortunate/*** = Pretty Good/** = Fair/* = Unsatisfactory

Career *

It won't be easy for Horses to handle their business affairs because they will face a lot of problems and challenges throughout the year. Horses have to put in extra time and effort at work, or they can hardly achieve any important breakthroughs in their careers. Fortunately they will have enough energy and ability to overcome almost all of their hardships by year end if they refuse to give up midway through. Horses will have better opportunities at work during the first, fifth, sixth, ninth and the last month; they should try to make good use of these months if they wish to have a better year for themselves. Besides this, Horses must keep alert to watch out for possible oncoming troubles and disputes, and try to settle them before they get out of control.

Money * *

This will not be a fortunate year for Horses, so they should try to be very conservative in money affairs. This means they must take extra precautions for their investments during the second, third, seventh and eighth month. On the other hand, Horses will have better luck in money affairs during the first, fifth, sixth and the last month of the year. One thing Horses should keep in mind is that they must try to save more money for the rainy days to come within the year.

Health * * *

The health of Horses will be pretty good this year. They will be in good shape both physically and mentally, but they should try not to indulge themselves too much in sex and alcohol, or their health will be spoiled. It's very important for Horses to get enough rest and sleep during the second, fourth, seventh and tenth month. It's not worthwhile for them to lose their health for anything else. Apart from this, Horses must try to avoid being hurt on the streets either as a result of traffic accidents or street violence during the third month. Most important of all, Horses must watch their home safety carefully, particularly during the fourth and fifth month.

Love ****

Horses will be able to enjoy a very romantic year. They will have better luck in love affairs during the first, fourth, tenth and the last month. However, they may probably face certain problems in their love affairs during the third, sixth, eighth and the eleventh month. Horses will be busily engaged in different social activities and will become key figures on these occasions, but they must watch their words and behaviour during the ninth month or they will encounter endless troubles in the following months.

According to traditional Chinese astrology, the distributions of the Lucky and Unlucky Stars within a Sign will more or less determine a person's fate in a particular year. Just as the distributions of the Stars change from year to year, however, they also change from month to month. Each Sign's fate for the year and for each month is calculated according to this basic rule.

Monthly In-Depth Forecasts
The First Month (4 February – 4 March)

The early bird catches the worm

This is one the most favourable months of the year for Horses, so they should try to make good use of this period of time or they will miss several good chances. Horses should try to go out to contact their prospective clients instead of waiting passively in their offices. Sensibility and diligence will be the two wings of their success; Horses must keep this in mind throughout the month.

It would be much better for Horses to stay one step ahead at work; by doing so they will surely succeed. If they fail to do so, the story will be completely different.

This will be a very romantic month for Horses. However, they should try not to let their busy social lives occupy too much of their time, or their careers might suffer.

Horses will be quite fortunate in money affairs this month. They will have some luck with lotteries and gambling, and they will be able to get satisfactory returns from their investments too.

The Second Month (5 March – 4 April)

Delays are dangerous

The fortune of Horses will drop sharply this month. They will face different problems and disputes at work within this period, and they'll have to put in extra time and effort to settle them. It would be much better if Horses can take action sooner rather than later, because things will get out of control if they fail to do so. Horses should keep in mind that 'Delays are dangerous.' Probably, their opponents will try to take advantage of any delay. Apart from this, hesitation in taking chances will be another serious handicap to Horses' success within the month.

This month is definitely not a profitable period for Horses. Because of the appearance of several Unlucky Stars within the Sign, Horses will be the big losers if they try their luck at gambling or high-risk investments. They should never get involved in any loans within this period, or there will be endless troubles for them in the months to come.

Horses will be pretty weak physically, so they should try to get enough rest and sleep to prevent a serious illness. In addition, they must try not to indulge in sex and drugs.

The Third Month (5 April – 4 May)

A burnt child dreads fire

The fortune of Horses won't see any improvement this month, so they should keep alert in watching out for potential problems and dangers. They must handle their business with extreme care in order to avoid a serious mistake. Horses should never play with fire at work, or they will get burnt. It would be much better if Horses can avoid serious conflict with their superiors within this period.

There will be sex temptations this month. Unless Horses can keep themselves calm enough to keep away, they will get seriously burnt. Apart from this, Horses must watch out for their road safety – that means they must walk and drive carefully at night within this period.

The fortune of Horses in money affairs will be going up and down like a roller coaster this month. It would be wise for them to be conservative in handling their money affairs, and they should keep in mind that 'A penny saved is a penny earned.'

The Fourth Month (5 May – 4 June)

Every cloud has its silver lining

Horses should try not to give up at this stage because things are getting better and better for them at work. It would be a pity if they are tired out under the continuous pressure of their heavy workload. Determination will be the key factor of the Horse's survival this year. Horses can create a miracle within this period if they show enough strong determination. Apart from this, Horses should try to upgrade their tools and equipment at work this month. This will enable them to beat their opponents in the months to come.

Although their health is improving, Horses should try to get enough rest and sleep to avoid a breakdown physically and mentally. In addition, Horses should keep alert in watching out for their home safety. They must pay special attention in taking care of their children to make sure that they go nowhere near ladders or windows to avoid a sudden big fall.

There will be some breakthroughs in love for Horses this month. But they should try not to be too picky in dealing with their lovers and friends, or they will be very sorry very soon.

The Fifth Month (5 June – 6 July)

If you can't beat them, join them

Horses will be quite successful if they can reach a compromise with their partner, clients or superiors during this period. It would be much better for Horses if they can settle any legal problems as soon as possible. A long legal procedure will hurt their careers and economic affairs very badly. Most important of all, Horses should reconsider their situation carefully and try to make some adjustments if necessary. For instance, if their competitors are too strong for them, then they have to think about joining them for self-preservation. If they are reluctant to do so, Horses should at least try to form an alliance with people in the same trade. Horses should keep in mind that combining forces is very important for their careers during this period.

This is one of the most fortunate months in money affairs for Horses. They will glean an income from different sources. However, they should watch out for fire at home or their valuables will be badly damaged.

Horses will be quite healthy this month, but they have to watch out for their personal safety when they are on any journeys. They must try not to be left alone in foreign or strange places.

The Sixth Month (7 July – 6 August)

A wise man will make more opportunities than he finds

Horses' situation becomes much better this month, so they should try to keep their eyes wide open to watch out for oncoming opportunities. They will be very successful if they can grasp some of these in time. However, it would be much better if Horses try to create chances for themselves actively instead of just waiting for them to come along. It takes some sense and cleverness to create chances, but Horses will be wise enough to do so during this period of time. If somebody invites them into a joint venture in a new business, it's worthwhile considering it in detail now.

Horses should not be too over-confident in love affairs because there will be some other people trying to challenge them during this period. It's very important for Horses to show their affection to their loved ones in time, before it's too late.

The fortune of Horses in money affairs will be pretty good this month. However, they have to watch their expenses because it's better for them to save for the rainy days ahead in the coming months.

The Seventh Month (7 August – 6 September)

Old habits die hard

It's time for Horses to make the corrections necessary for personal and professional success. They should try to find out if there are any weaknesses or loopholes about. If Horses are able to make the repair works on time, they will be in a much better position to deal with competitors and opponents, not only this month but in the months to come. As the old saying goes, 'Old habits die hard.' Horses will find that making changes will be quite difficult. Their success at work, however, will depend on their own determination. The advice and assistance from good friends and partners will be a big help to them in this matter.

Horses should try to kick old habits in their personal lives too. If possible, Horses must not indulge too much in sex and alcohol. Most important of all, a taste of drugs during this period will lead to total destruction.

The fortune of Horses in money affairs will drop sharply at the end of the month. Therefore, they should try not to risk their money in gambling, or they will lose more money than they ever anticipated.

The Eighth Month (7 September – 7 October)

It's no use crying over spilled milk

Horses may suffer a serious defeat in their career this month. But it's no use crying over spilled milk. What they should do at this stage is try to make a recovery as soon as possible. An objective analysis of their business will help them to find the most effective remedy for themselves. Asking for professional advice from experts would be an effective solution. No matter what happens, Horses should insist on performing their duties and should never give up under pressure. Apart from this, Horses should try to keep their business secret, and shouldn't talk too much about it in public. If they do, they will receive another serious blow at work.

This month is definitely not a profitable period for Horses because of the appearance of several Unlucky Stars within their Sign. They must keep their eyes wide open and try to keep away from money traps.

Horses may face a broken relationship with their lovers during this period if over the past few months they have been reluctant to show their care and affection. However, they should not be too sorry about this and should just let bygones be bygones.

The Ninth Month (8 October – 6 November)

The harder you work, the luckier you get

Horses will see some important breakthroughs in business this month, but they should work even harder so they achieve even better results in the coming months. However, Horses should make sure that they are working for the right target, or all their efforts will be wasted. It would be much better for them to evaluate their work from time to time throughout the month. Horses will have some good news from foreign countries this month, and they may have a better chance of success if they start their overseas business this month.

If they are looking for a loan, Horses will be able to get the necessary approval now. Horses should not, however, try to buy property or valuables that are far beyond their financial means, or they will be in big trouble in the years to come.

Horses will be busily engaged in different social activities, and they will be quite popular among their new acquaintances. However, they must mind their speech at these occasions to avoid unnecessary personal disputes.

The Tenth Month (7 November – 6 December)

There are tricks in every trade

Horses should keep their eyes wide open to watch out for dirty tricks played by their opponents this month. They will be badly defeated if they overlook them. If somebody asks them along on a joint venture in a new business, Horses must study the whole thing in detail very carefully in order to avoid falling into business traps. Apart from this, Horses should try not to get involved in any business they are unfamiliar with. They will lose a lot of money if they don't know too much about the tricks of that particular business. It would be much better for Horses to stay in their own positions for the time being.

Health is turning bad towards the end of the month. Horses must take care over the cleanliness of their food, or they will suffer very much from stomach ache or even food poisoning. It's much better to be safe than sorry.

Horses have to try to use some tricks to impress their lovers this month. A little trick during this period will be much more effective than thousands of words. Probably, this little trick will also leave them and their lovers with an unforgettable memory.

The Eleventh Month (7 December – 4 January)

Of two evils, choose the lesser

This will be one of the most unfavourable months of the year for Horses. They will face strong challenges at work during this time. Unless they can handle them with extreme care, Horses will end up helpless victims of their opponents. Worst of all, Horses will find that they are caught in a dilemma and totally confused. They must try to make a quick choice even though it might be very difficult for them to do so. 'Of two evils, choose the lesser.' Horses should keep this in mind in making their decisions.

This month is definitely not a good time for Horses to start any new projects or new business, so they should turn down all these kinds of offers or invitations firmly during this period.

Horses will probably have to make a choice in their love affairs. It would be much better if they can ask the advice of elders or good friends before they make their final decision. No matter what happens, Horses should keep calm and try not to provoke anyone involved.

The fortune of Horses will be at one of its lowest ebbs this month. Their monthly income might be endangered during this period. Worst of all, there will be many unexpected expenses for Horses, and they will be in big trouble if they haven't saved enough money for themselves over previous months.

The Twelfth Month (5 January – 3 February)

When things are at the worst, they begin to mend

Although this won't be a very fortunate year for Horses, they will see some breakthroughs in their career at the end of the year after all their struggles. However, the story will be very different if Horses have failed to put in the extra time and effort in their work throughout the year. Strong determination and aggressive action together will contribute to their eventual success. Horses will find that the difficulties and challenges of last month will fade away gradually now. They will be able to carry out their work freely without these extra heavy burdens.

The fortune of Horses in money affairs will be much improved this month. Financial crises will be all over at the beginning of the month, but they should think about saving for the rainy days to come in the future. It would be much better if Horses can keep away from gambling and high-risk investments for the time being.

Horses should try to spend more time with their lovers, and show their care and affection to them from time and time. It would be quite dangerous if they play with fire and cheat on them.

Using Feng Shui to Improve Fortune: Directions, Colours, Numbers and Lucky Charm

The ancient Chinese used the traditional Horoscope to predict their fortune on a yearly basis – they used the art of Feng Shui to improve their luck.

It was their belief that the application of tactical Feng Shui would change their bad luck into good, and make their good luck improve even more.

This same method is still effective in today's modern world.

There are four main elements which I will use in tactical Feng Shui:

- ◆ Lucky Directions
- ◆ Lucky Colours
- ◆ Lucky Numbers
- ◆ Lucky Charm

Horses have to struggle very hard if they want to have any break-throughs in studies and business. They should not indulge themselves too much, or they will miss many good chances. This will not be a fortunate year for Horses, so they should try to be very conservative in money affairs. Fortunately, Horses will be in pretty good shape physically and mentally. They will also enjoy a very romantic year. They will be very popular among new acquaintances.

I would suggest applying the following Feng Shui tactics to improve luck so that Horses don't have to worry too much about their fate within the year.

Lucky Directions

The most favourable directions of the year for the Horse are **South**, **Southwest** and **Northeast**. Horses should sleep or sit in these directions if they wish to improve their fortune.

To make this procedure very simple, divide the house or room into nine imaginary squares. Then, using a compass, check the exact direction of each square as shown in Figure 2. This will help to ensure that you do not make a mistake with the direction.

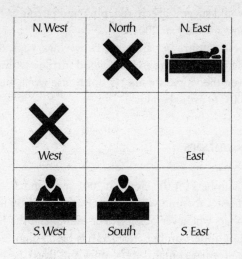

N. West	North	N. East
	✕	🛏
✕		
West		East
🧑	🧑	
S. West	South	S. East

Figure 2

The Horse should sit in the relevant directions at work or while studying; this will ensure that their achievements are much greater than the Stars intended. To improve health and achieve a good night's sleep, position your bed in the favourable direction shown (Northeast).

However, the Horse should try to keep away from the unfavourable directions of the year; that is, West and North as shown in Figure 2. The Horse should try not to sit, work or sleep in these directions, so as to get rid of the negative influences lurking there.

Lucky Colours

According to Chinese tradition, each of the five elements has its own representative colours. Fire is represented by red, pink and purple, Earth by yellow and brown, and so on. As a Feng Shui

Master I would suggest **green**, **red**, **pink** and **purple** as the Horse's lucky colours for the year 2001.

Use these colours in paints, wall coverings, rugs, drapes and curtains. This will be sure to bring good fortune within the year.

However, the Horse should try not to use white, blue, grey or black in 2001, to avoid bad luck.

Lucky Numbers

The lucky numbers for the Horse in 2001 are: **1** and **5**.

The Horse's fortune will be much improved by using these lucky numbers whenever possible. For example, if the Horse has a choice, the phone number 215-1551 is better than 286-4262 – because the former contains more ones and fives, the Horse's two lucky numbers for the year.

Lucky Charm

Feng Shui Masters believe that special objects can be used as a medium between human beings and nature. The fortune of the recipient is greatly improved as the positive wave of energy from nature is passed through the object or 'lucky charm' on to the recipient.

The lucky charm for the Horse in 2001 is a brown stone carving of three goats walking out from a stone, as shown below. There's a Chinese character '泰' inscribed on top of the stone. For the best result, this stone carving should be placed in the south or the northeast direction of the house.

_____

Chapter Three

The
Sheep

Years of the Sheep

1907 (5/Feb/07—4/Feb/08)   1955 (4/Feb/55—4/Feb/56)
1919 (5/Feb/19—4/Feb/20)   1967 (4/Feb/67—4/Feb/68)
1931 (5/Feb/31—4/Feb/32)   1979 (4/Feb/79—4/Feb/80)
1943 (5/Feb/43—4/Feb/44)   1991 (4/Feb/91—3/Feb/92)

Distribution of the Stars within the Sign for 2001

Lucky Stars   **Unlucky Stars**

None   Leopard's Tail
Funeral's Door

Unlucky Stars
Leopard's Tail

The Chinese consider leopards to be among the fiercest animals in the jungle, who can cause a lot of trouble to those who happen to get in their way or step on their tails.

If this Star appears within the Sign it is best to be cautious, careful, discreet and maintain a low profile to avoid provoking anyone or arousing trouble.

Funeral's Door

In ancient China, funeral ceremonies were held at home. A pair of white lanterns were hung outside to announce the death. The front door was kept closed to prevent unnecessary disturbances by those unconnected with the funeral. Since then, a tightly closed door with a pair of white lanterns has symbolized a grief-stricken family.

When this Star appears, people have to take care of their elderly family members by making sure that they receive the proper medical treatments when required. In addition, they should pay more attention to their home safety.

General Overview of the Year

This will be a pretty rough year for Sheep because of the appearance of the Unlucky Stars within their Sign. This year is definitely not a good time for them to start any important new projects, or they will end up with nothing after long struggling. Sheep should try to keep a low profile, and never try to challenge their superiors, or they will become a sure loser eventually.

The fortune of Sheep in money affairs will fluctuate from time to time throughout the year so that they should keep alert to being 'money wise' and try to keep away from money traps.

Sheep will be quite weak physically this year, so they must take care of themselves.

It will be quite difficult for Sheep to keep their lovers unless they show their care and affection to them soon enough in the year.

Career	*
Money	**
Health	*
Love	**

** = Fair/* = Unsatisfactory

Career *

Sheep will face different kinds of difficulties at work this year, so it would be much better for them not to carry out new projects or start new business ventures within this period of time. Otherwise they might be very disappointed to find out that they end up with nothing after long struggling. In order to survive in business, Sheep must put more time and effort in at work during the first, fourth, fifth, sixth and the last month. Most important of all, Sheep should try to keep a low profile and try not to challenge or provoke their superiors or they will become helpless victims eventually. However, Sheep will have better opportunities at work during the second, third and tenth month. Sheep should try to make good use of these months if they wish to see better achievement at year end.

Money **

The fortune of Sheep in money affairs will fluctuate from time to time throughout the year. Consequently they should not risk their money in gambling and investments, particularly during the first, sixth and eighth month. However, Sheep will have better luck in money affairs during the second and seventh month. Generally speaking, Sheep should be money wise and keep away from money traps throughout the year. On the seventh month they should try not to lend their money out because it will prove quite difficult for them to get their money back later on.

Health *

Sheep will be pretty weak physically this year. They have to watch out for their health carefully, or they could end up in hospital. Sheep have to pay special attention to their health during the third, fourth, eighth, ninth and also the last two months of the year. On the sixth month, Sheep must keep away from water and seafood. Apart from this, Sheep should watch out for the health and safety of their elder family members during the fifth month. Sheep should keep well away from drugs throughout the year, or they will be very sorry later on.

Love **

Sheep should not expect too much from romance this year. They'll find nary a trace of true love even though there will be a lot of people about. Having said this, they will have better luck during the fifth and the eleventh month. Unless Sheep can give up their self-righteous attitude towards their lovers, they will face a broken relationship near the year end.

According to traditional Chinese astrology, the distributions of the Lucky and Unlucky Stars within a Sign will more or less determine a person's fate in a particular year. Just as the distributions of the Stars change from year to year, however, they also change from month to month. Each Sign's fate for the year and for each month is calculated according to this basic rule.

Monthly In-depth Forecasts
The First Month (4 February – 4 March)
It's a poor heart that never rejoices

This will be one of the most unfavourable months of the year for Sheep. They must try to keep an optimistic and positive outlook in handling their very complicated work, or they will be badly defeated by their opponents. In other words, their faint heart will be the major handicap to the progress of their business. It would be a big help if Sheep can have someone to encourage them to face difficulties within this period. Apart from this, Sheep should never try to challenge or provoke their superiors or the people with authority this month in order to avoid extra trouble and pressures. Moderation will make things smooth without too many conflicts.

Although Sheep will be quite healthy within this period, they should keep a careful eye on their emotions. They tend to be quite moody this month. They should keep in mind that they are the only ones who can help themselves out of depression and sorrows. No one else can do this for them.

This month is definitely not a profitable period for Sheep, so it would not be wise for them to try their luck at gambling and high-risk investments. Apart from this, Sheep should also try to cut out unnecessary expenses as much as possible.

The Second Month (5 March – 4 April)

Do not throw pearls before swine

The fortune of Sheep will be much improved this month. That means Sheep will be quite productive at work if they are willing to put more effort into their business. Apart from this, Sheep will become quite persuasive within this period, so that this will be the right time for them to sell their ideas and proposals. However, they should not waste too much time in dealing with people who are ignorant and arrogant. Throwing pearls before swine leads only to total waste.

The fortune of Sheep in money affairs will be pretty good this month. Their loans will be approved, and there will be some unexpected income in the middle of the month. This is a (rare) good time for Sheep to buy property or valuables if they really want to do so.

It's probably time for Sheep to give up on a hopeless romance. It's just a waste of time if they keep on trying to win appreciation and love from uninterested others.

The Third Month (5 April – 4 May)

Everybody's business is nobody's business

Sheep will be quite productive this month, but there will be personal disputes within this period. Sheep have to try to settle these as soon as possible, or this month will be full of irrational arguments and quarrels, and this will prove too much for them. However, the major concern of Sheep is to take their responsibilities fully on themselves. Just as the old saying goes, if Sheep want something done well, they should do it themselves. A job will be totally spoiled if they wait for others to do it for them. Now's the time for Sheep to think about their future, but they should try to keep their plans top secret for the time being.

The health of Sheep is not so good this month, so they should try to get enough rest and sleep to avoid a sudden collapse physically and mentally. Apart from this, Sheep should watch out carefully for their home safety near the end of the month.

Sheep will be bothered by gossips and rumour this month. The best way forward is to try to keep calm, and keep a low profile. All of the gossip and rumour will eventually fade away.

The Fourth Month (5 May – 4 June)

Hasty climbers have sudden falls

Different kinds of troubles will arise one after another within this period, so that Sheep should try to keep calm while looking for effective solutions. Losing patience will mess everything up. Just as the old saying goes, 'Hasty climbers have sudden falls.' Sheep should not make hasty decisions. In other words, waiting patiently for a suitable time will enable them to pass through the hardships without too much damage. Most important of all, Sheep must try to keep up good personal relationships with their partners and subordinates through mutual understanding. Isolation without any source of support or help will be the most serious threat to Sheep's career this month.

Although Sheep will be busily engaged in numerous social activities, loneliness will follow after them like a shadow. They should give up their egocentric attitude if they want to become popular again.

The health of Sheep will be quite weak if they can't give up their heavy smoking and drinking. A taste of drugs within this period will lead them to destruction, so they must firmly say 'No' to this kind of temptation.

The Fifth Month (5 June – 6 July)

Knowledge is power

Last month's difficulties at work still linger, but Sheep will be able to handle them with more confidence and capability this month. First of all, however, Sheep must be willing to accept the advice of superiors and experts, and to pick up more knowledge about their jobs. Otherwise, their arrogance and ignorance will blind them and make them stumble on their way towards success. They should keep in mind that 'knowledge is power.' The more knowledge they pick up during this period, the more successful they will be in their future developments.

Sheep should watch out for the health and safety of an elderly family member this month. They must make sure that the old man or woman will be able to have proper medical treatment whenever needed, or they will end up very sorry.

There will be some breakthroughs in love for Sheep. They should never take love for granted. Their negligence about showing affection to their lover will hurt a delicate relationship very much. Sheep must not be reluctant to say sorry to their lover within this period if they have to do so.

The Sixth Month (7 July – 6 August)

Big fish eat little fish

Sheep have to try to protect themselves from being swallowed up by some other people within this period. Dangers and traps abound this month, so Sheep must keep their eyes wide open to avoid possible problems, and should try to settle any disputes as soon as possible. Any delays will be dangerous. Sheep will face severe challenges from strong opponents, and should bear in mind that 'Big fish eat little fish.' Surviving such a situation will be the Sheep's major concern this month. Joining forces with others to fight against the big fish is probably the best way forward.

This month is definitely not a good time for Sheep to try their luck at high-risk investments because of the appearance of several Unlucky Stars within their Sign. If they ignore this advice, they will be in big trouble in the months to come. Sheep should keep the old saying, 'Out of debt, out of trouble' in mind.

Sheep must keep away from seafood this month to avoid food poisoning. Apart from this, they should try to keep away from water too. Never swim or dive alone, especially in the middle of the month.

The Seventh Month (7 August – 6 September)

When in Rome, do as the Romans do

Although the fortune of Sheep will be improved a little bit this month, they still have to fight very hard for their survival in business. They should never try to play tricks this month, or they will fool nobody else but themselves. They have to follow the game's rules strictly if they don't want to be kicked out. Trying to keep in tune with circumstances at work will be the Sheep's major concern this month. Their future development will proceed much better if they are able to do so.

Sheep will probably become the focus of many social gatherings. However, they should keep this old saying in mind: 'When in Rome, do as the Romans do.' They will not only rid themselves of trouble but also win appreciation and popularity by doing so.

The fortune of Sheep in money affairs will be on an upward trend during this period. If they would like to ask for a loan, this would be a suitable time to do so. However, they should try not to lend money, or they will never see it again.

The Eighth Month (7 September – 7 October)

He who would eat the fruit must climb the tree

Sheep will be deeply disappointed about their business this month if they rely too much upon others to carry out their work. Sheep have to keep in mind that they have to climb the tree if they want to eat the fruit. Apart from this, Sheep should try to keep alert to prevent being cheated or betrayed by the people around them, or they will be in deep trouble. There will probably be some people asking them in on a joint venture in business or investment. Unfortunately, this is not a good time for Sheep to enter into any such arrangement.

The fortune of Sheep will be on a downward trend towards the end of the month, so they should mind their finances if they don't want to suffer money problems. They will have some luck in lottery and gambling at the beginning of the month, but they will become a big loser if they keep on trying their luck in the latter part of the month.

Sheep will be quite weak physically and mentally this month. They should not hesitate to see the doctor for a check-up or treatment if there is something wrong with them. Their own house will provide a comfortable shelter for them this month, so they should spend more time at home with their family members.

The Ninth Month (8 October – 6 November)

What cannot be cured must be endured

This month is one of the most difficult periods for Sheep. They will face severe challenges and criticism during this month, and they have to try their best to handle the situation properly and not let it get out of control. If some serious misery takes place, Sheep should try to control themselves to avoid a nervous breakdown. The earlier they emerge from their grief, the better shape they'll be in to face the future. They must bear in mind this old saying: 'What cannot be cured must be endured.' Sheep should try to be realistic and practical; they must forget about their misfortunes and face reality as soon as possible. This month is definitely not a good time for them to take a vacation; they must on the contrary put extra time and effort into handling their business.

No matter how busy they are, Sheep must try to get enough rest and sleep this month. Home safety is the major concern of the month. Sheep will be very sorry if they ignore the health and safety of elders at home.

Probably, Sheep will face a broken relationship with their lovers this month. If this happens, Sheep should not bury themselves in grief or bitterness. Let bygones be bygones. There's no use crying over spilled milk.

The Tenth Month (7 November – 6 December)

It is better to give than to receive

This is one of the most fortunate months in money affairs for Sheep. Their money problems of previous months will be solved eventually, and they will be much relieved now. However, Sheep should not hesitate to help those people who really are in financial difficulty. Their assistance will not only help others, but will bring some unexpected rewards to them in the near future. 'It is better to give than to receive.' Sheep should keep this old saying in mind this month. Last month's business misfortunes will clear away gradually this month, so that Sheep should try to make good use of this period for developing plans for the future. Sheep will become the focus of attention at the office, and it's time for them to demonstrate their creativity and capability. However, Sheep should try to be humble enough to communicate and exchange ideas with their subordinates. Doing so will result in a pleasant surprise.

The health of Sheep will be much improved. This month is a good time for them to take a vacation. They will be much refreshed physically and mentally by the time they get back.

The Eleventh Month (7 December – 4 January)

Faint heart never won fair lady

Sheep will become quite passionate this month. Although they are eagerly looking for a true love within this period, they tend to be reluctant to show their affection. Unless they have the guts to express their true feelings, Sheep will miss a very good opportunity. Just as the old saying goes, 'Faint heart never won fair lady.' Sheep should encourage themselves to take action before it is too late.

Sheep should have the same courage in their career. They will be quite successful if they have the guts to demonstrate their talent and ability to their superiors and clients. Most important of all, Sheep should try to keep their promises, or they will lose the necessary support from the people around them.

Sheep will be under the threat of infection continuously within this period, so it's necessary for them to take care of themselves. They should try to keep away from unhygienic food and crowded places, or they might end up in hospital.

The Twelfth Month (5 January – 3 February)

The darkest hour is just before dawn

Different difficulties and disputes will come up one after another within this period, so it's necessary for Sheep to keep a positive and aggressive attitude at work and never say die. Just as the old saying goes, 'The darkest hour is just before dawn.' Things will move in their favour if they can insist on carrying out their duties. No matter what happens, Sheep should try to keep a low profile to avoid provoking anyone in authority or stirring up trouble. If possible, Sheep should ask for the advice and permission of their superiors before they carry out any important projects.

The health of Sheep will be at a low ebb this month. They must try to get enough rest and sleep so they don't exhaust themselves under the pressure of their heavy workload. Apart from this, they should pay special attention to home safety. Particularly, they should watch out for fire at home.

Unless Sheep can give up their self-righteous attitude towards their lovers, they will face a broken relationship this month. However, there may be some breakthrough in a love affair next month if they begin to show their care and affection.

Using Feng Shui to Improve Fortune: Directions, Colours, Numbers and Lucky Charm

The ancient Chinese used the traditional Horoscope to predict their fortune on a yearly basis – they used the art of Feng Shui to improve their luck.

It was their belief that the application of tactical Feng Shui would change their bad luck into good, and make their good luck improve even more.

This same method is still effective in today's modern world.

There are four main elements which I will use in tactical Feng Shui:

- ◆ Lucky Directions
- ◆ Lucky Colours
- ◆ Lucky Numbers
- ◆ Lucky Charm

This will not be a very good year for Sheep, so they should not start any important new projects; otherwise they will end up with nothing after a long struggle. Most important of all, Sheep should keep a low profile to avoid provoking their superiors. Sheep's fortune will fluctuate from time to time throughout the year. This year is definitely not a good time for them to buy property. They are physically weak, so they should watch their health carefully. Besides this, they should take good care of elderly family members too. Sheep will have a hard time finding true love even though there will be a lot of opportunities around them.

I would suggest applying the following Feng Shui tactics to improve luck so that Sheep don't have to worry too much about their fate within the year.

Lucky Directions

The most favourable directions of the year for Sheep are **South**, **North** and **Northwest**. Sheep should sleep or sit in these directions if they wish to improve their fortune.

To make this procedure very simple, divide the house or room into nine imaginary squares. Then, using a compass, check the exact direction of each square as shown in Figure 3. This will help to ensure that you do not make a mistake with the direction.

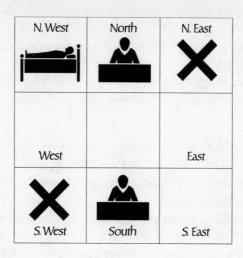

N. West	North	N. East
West		East
S. West	South	S. East

Figure 3

Sheep should sit in the relevant directions at work or while study-ing; this will ensure that their achievements are much greater than the Stars intended. To improve health and achieve a good night's sleep, Sheep should position their bed in the favourable direction shown (Northwest).

However, Sheep should try to keep away from the unfav-ourable directions of the year; that is, Southwest and Northeast as shown in Figure 3. Sheep should try not to sit, work or sleep in these directions, in order to get rid of the negative influences lurking there.

Lucky Colours

According to Chinese tradition, each of the five elements has its own representative colours. Fire is represented by red, pink and purple, Earth by yellow and brown, and so on. As a Feng Shui

Master I would suggest **green** and **white** as Sheep's lucky colours for the year 2001.

Use these colours in paints, wall coverings, rugs, drapes and curtains. This will be sure to bring good fortune within the year.

However, Sheep should try not to use blue, grey, black, yellow or brown in 2001, to avoid bad luck.

Lucky Numbers

The lucky numbers for Sheep in 2001 are: **6** and **9**.

Fortune will be much improved by using these lucky numbers whenever possible. For example, if Sheep has a choice, the phone number 269-9269 is better than 251-5311 – because the former contains more sixes and nines, Sheep's two lucky numbers for the year.

Lucky Charm

Feng Shui Masters believe that special objects can be used as a medium between human beings and nature. The fortune of the recipient is greatly improved as the positive wave of energy from nature is passed through the object or 'lucky charm' on to the recipient.

The lucky charm for the Sheep in 2001 is a pair of kylin with ganoderma in their mouth and a pearl in between their two front legs, as shown below. The scales on their bodies look like the traditional Chinese coins. For the best result, they should be placed in the north or the northwest direction of the house.

Chapter Four

The
Monkey

Years of the Monkey

1908 (5/Feb/08—3/Feb/09) 1956 (5/Feb/56—3/Feb/57)
1920 (5/Feb/20—3/Feb/21) 1968 (5/Feb/68—3/Feb/69)
1932 (5/Feb/32—3/Feb/33) 1980 (5/Feb/80—3/Feb/81)
1944 (5/Feb/44—3/Feb/45) 1992 (4/Feb/92—3/Feb/93)

Distribution of the Stars within the Sign for 2001

Lucky Stars	Unlucky Stars
The Moon	Sudden Death
Union of the Year	God of Loneliness
	God of Death
	Tightened Loop
	Hooked and Strained

Lucky Stars
The Moon

The concept of Yin (female) and Yang (male) is very strong in Chinese culture. Just as the Sun symbolized Yang, the Moon for centuries has symbolized Yin.

The appearance of this Star is a good omen because it will brighten up life just as the Moon brightens up the world at night.

Union of the Year

Unity is important for success. In the Chinese Horoscope, this Star harmonizes well with the year. Its appearance is a very good omen.

When this Star appears, people will be very popular and find it easy to win the friendship and support of those around them. Such good relations will bring handsome rewards in different projects and investments.

Unlucky Stars
Sudden Death

Due to the inadequate knowledge of medicine in ancient China, a lot of sudden deaths were believed to be caused by the unpredictable will of the gods. This kind of ignorance kept many from trying to get medical care when they needed it.

This Star is one of the worst Unlucky Stars in the Chinese Horoscope. When this Star appears within a Sign, people have to keep all medical appointments and try to take preventative measures before it is too late.

God of Loneliness

In traditional Chinese society, living happily and harmoniously with other family members and friends was considered to be a great blessing. On the other hand, to live alone or to be ostracized by family or society was considered a horrible fate.

When this Star appears, people need to work on improving

their relations with relatives, friends and colleagues, or they may be isolated.

God of Death

This is definitely the least propitious Star in the Chinese Horoscope. It is named after Wang Shen, the God of Death, who the ancient Chinese believed had control over a person's mortality.

The Star's appearance is a very bad omen, a warning to take extreme care, avoid risks and always follow the motto 'safety first.'

Tightened Loop

Loops were commonly used by the ancient Chinese to catch animals. Consequently, a loop is usually considered to be the symbol of a trap. A person, as well as an animal, might get caught or even strangled by a tightened loop. So it is better to stay away from any kind of traps.

The appearance of this Star is a warning signal. People have to keep their eyes wide open to watch out for the traps in front of them. Otherwise, it will prove very difficult to get out of the traps and dilemmas.

Hooked and Strained

Being hooked by sharp objects or strained by ropes are definitely very terrible experiences. Unfortunately, this Star is somewhat related with these two dire events.

The appearance of this Star is a bad omen. People have to be very careful every step of the way in order to avoid risking their within the year.

General Overview of the Year

Although this will not be a very successful year for Monkeys, they will enjoy a pretty happy and smooth life with their friends, relatives and colleagues. Monkeys will have numerous difficulties at the beginning of the year, but they should never give up. These difficulties will be solved more easily and effectively with compromise rather than confrontation. It would be much better if Monkeys can settle their personal disputes as quickly as possible. In addition to their steady income, Monkeys will have luck in lottery and gambling, but they should try not to be too greedy.

Monkeys have to watch out for their personal safety when they travel. It will be quite possible for Monkeys to enjoy a sweet relationship with their lovers this year, but they should try to keep their promises and never cheat on them.

Career	**
Money	****
Health	**
Love	****

**** = Very Fortunate/** = Fair

Career **

Monkeys will face a lot of difficulties at the beginning of the year, however things will get better and better towards year end. Therefore, Monkeys should never give up and should try to fight to the finish if they don't want their careers to be fruitless this year. Harmony is the key to success this year. This means that if Monkeys can keep up good relations with the people around them, they will have a much better chance of achieving their goals. They should keep in mind that compromise is much better than confrontation when it comes to problem-solving this year. Personal disputes will hurt their business seriously, so they must try to settle them as soon as possible. However, Monkeys will have better opportunities at work during the third, fourth, sixth, tenth and eleventh month. They will be more successful if they can try to make use of these five months.

Money * * * *

Financially, Monkeys need not to worry about money this year because they will have an abundant and steady income. In addition to this, Monkeys will have luck in occasional lottery and gambling this year. The most fortunate months of the year for Monkeys will be the third, fourth, sixth and ninth. However, Monkeys must try not to show off their money or possessions to avoid a robbery or break-in during the first, sixth and the last month of the year. Most important of all, Monkeys might have financial problems during the tenth month if they fail to save money in months previous.

Health * *

Monkeys will be quite healthy in the first half of the year, but the situation will deteriorate towards year end. The months during which they have to watch their health very carefully are the third, seventh, tenth and eleventh. Apart from this, Monkeys have to keep on watching out for the danger of fire during the first and fifth month. In addition, Monkeys must try to watch out for their personal safety when they travel or hunt during the third, eighth and the tenth month.

Love * * * *

Monkeys will enjoy a sweet relationship with their lovers this year. A struggling relationship will improve, and probably there will be a rebirth of a dying love. However, Monkeys will face certain problems in love affairs during the second, fourth and seventh month. There will be numerous rumours and gossip about their romance, but Monkeys should keep calm and take it easy because almost all of them will be gone with the wind very soon. Most important of all, Monkeys should try their best to keep their promises and never cheat on their lovers, or they will face a very terrible and sad ending.

According to traditional Chinese astrology, the distributions of the Lucky and Unlucky Stars within a Sign will more or less determine a person's fate in a particular year. Just as the distributions of the Stars change from year to year, however, they also change from month to month. Each Sign's fate for the year and for each month is calculated according to this basic rule.

Monthly In-depth Forecasts
The First Month (4 February – 4 March)

It never rains but it pours

There will be numerous difficulties and personal disputes coming one after another within this period. Monkeys should try to settle them before they get out of control. Monkeys can't afford to take any breaks in handling these matters because they will keep on coming during this month. However, they will have a much better chance of survival if they can maintain good personal and business relations within this period. One thing Monkeys should always keep in mind is that they must try to keep their word and promises, or their careers will be seriously hurt in the near future.

Although the health of Monkeys will be in pretty good shape this month, they must keep an eye on their personal safety. They should in particular keep away from fire.

The fortune of Monkeys will be going up and down like a roller-coaster this month, so they should never try their luck in gambling or high-risk investments. Apart from this, they must pay special attention to taking care of their money and valuables in order to avoid a theft or burglary.

The Second Month (5 March – 4 April)

Nothing is permanent but change

There will be several major changes for Monkeys this month, in both their personal and business life. They should keep their eyes wide open and try their best to keep up with the pace of change. If they cannot, they will be left far behind. One thing Monkeys should keep in mind is that they must try not to bind themselves to their old customs. They should make corresponding changes according to the demands of the situation if they want to survive.

Monkeys will face almost the same situation in their love affairs within this period. Probably, a third person will step in between their lovers and them, and make the situation complicated. Under these circumstances, Monkeys have to re-evaluate their relationships and try to take the corresponding action in order to strengthen themselves.

The fortune of Monkeys will fluctuate from time to time within this period. Consequently, they should try to be conservative in handling their money affairs to avoid a big loss.

The Third Month (5 April – 4 May)

Diligence is the mother of good fortune

This is one of the most favourable months of the year for Monkeys, so they should try to make good use of this period of time if they want to have a more successful year. Just as the old saying goes, 'Diligence is the mother of good fortune.' Monkeys have to work hard for themselves, or they will spoil several chances this month. Apart from this, Monkeys should try to reach a compromise with their clients or competitors, or they will face a lot of problems.

No matter how busy they are, Monkeys should try to have enough rest and sleep to avoid exhaustion. This month is definitely not a suitable time for them to take a vacation. However, if they have to make any journeys during this period, Monkeys have to keep an eye on the cleanliness of their food to avoid food poisoning.

This will be a very romantic month for Monkeys. They should not forget about family members, however, and should try to spend more time with them. This will provide an unforgettable memory for them in coming years.

The Fourth Month (5 May – 4 June)

Trust men and they will trust in you

Monkeys will become quite creative and capable this month, so they will be able to handle their business with ease. However, a good relationship will help them to be even more successful, so it's time for Monkeys to be friendly to others. They have to trust people if they wish to have more friends. Mutual trust and understanding are essential to a good relationship between Monkeys and their partners and clients during this period. This month will be a very good time for Monkeys to carry out new projects or to start a new business because they will face fewer obstacles than usual right now.

Monkeys tend to be suspicious this month. Many misunderstandings will therefore be aroused in their love affairs. Their major concern is to try to engender mutual trust with their lovers as soon as possible.

This is one of the most fortunate months in money affairs for Monkeys. They will have luck in lottery and gambling, but they should try not to be too greedy.

The Fifth Month (5 June – 6 July)

The saddest thing I can imagine is to get used to luxury

The fortune of Monkeys in money affairs will drop suddenly and sharply this month, a situation that will prove quite dangerous for them if they haven't prepared themselves beforehand. Monkeys tend to over-spend this month. It would be much better for them if they can cut out their luxurious and extravagant habits, or they will be in deep trouble in the months to come. Most important of all, Monkeys must not get involved in any loans, and should try to pay up all their bills as soon as possible.

Monkeys will face severe challenges at work during this period, so they should try to strengthen themselves psychologically and refuse to give up under any circumstances. Apart from this, Monkeys should try to mind their own business and should criticize nothing about the business of the other people.

The health condition of Monkeys will be quite good this month. However, they have to watch out carefully for their home safety, especially about fire at home.

The Sixth Month (7 July – 6 August)

Success grows from the struggle to overcome difficulties

Monkeys will be able to overcome their difficulties this month with the help of several Lucky Stars within their Sign. However, they have to work hard for their success because they won't get something for nothing. One thing for sure is that their efforts within this period will not be wasted, and will in fact pay off handsomely. However, Monkeys should try not to be blinded by their success, or they will suffer later on. They should try to be moderate in dealing with their colleagues and clients; by doing so they will get the necessary support in return.

The fortune of Monkeys in money affairs will be much improved this month. Their income will become more steady now. However, it's very important for them not to show off too much in order to avoid a robbery or break-in.

Monkeys will be busily engaged in different social activities, but must mind their words carefully to avoid unnecessary misunderstandings and trouble. Apart from this, they must try not to over-eat or over-drink at these social occasions.

The Seventh Month (7 August – 6 September)

Better to wear out than to rust away

This will be a very busy month at work for Monkeys. They will be under stress as a result of their heavy work schedule. However, Monkeys should never try to escape from their duties during this period, or they will miss a very good opportunity for promotion. Monkeys should not complain too much about their heavy workload, because it is just as the old saying goes, 'Better to wear out than to rust away.' If they let this opportunity slip through their fingers now, it won't come knocking again.

However, Monkeys must try to get enough rest and sleep this month in order to avoid a sudden breakdown physically or mentally. Indulging in sex and alcohol will surely make the situation even worse.

No matter what happens, Monkeys should try not to forget about their lovers. They should show their care and affection from time to time throughout the month in order to maintain intimacy. Even a telephone call or fax would be fine if Monkeys really cannot find time for dining out or spending time with their loved ones.

The Eighth Month (7 September – 7 October)

Self-preservation is the first law of nature

Rumour and gossip of all kinds dog Monkeys during this period. They should try to keep a low profile. It would be much better if Monkeys could walk away from the job for a while, perhaps by taking a vacation. If it is impossible for them to do so, they should try to keep their eyes down and their mouths closed – the necessary tactics for self-preservation this month. A strong alliance with colleagues is another effective solution. One important thing they should keep in mind is that they must never try to betray their colleagues or superiors in exchange for their own survival or success, because they will surely be found out and ostracized sooner or later in retribution.

Monkeys have to follow the rules of safety when they travel or hunt. They must keep alert to possible oncoming dangers.

It's definitely not a profitable month for Monkeys, so they should try not to risk their money in gambling. Most important of all, Monkeys have to keep their eyes wide open for money traps, or they will lose a lot of money.

The Ninth Month (8 October – 6 November)

You cannot catch old birds with chaff

Monkeys will probably come into conflict with experienced clients or opponents this month. It takes some cunning to deal with them effectively, so Monkeys will need a good plan beforehand. Otherwise, they will become the loser of the game. First of all, Monkeys must try to equip themselves with better knowledge and more money, so they will become unbeatable in these confrontations. Apart from this, Monkeys should try to be punctual in all business meetings and appointments, or their opponents will take advantage and deal them a serious blow. Monkeys must keep in mind that they can't fool anybody with empty words or promises during this period, so it would be much better for them stop so at once.

Although the fortune of Monkeys will be much improved this month, they should reconsider their investments during this period. They must keep in mind that any investments they make at this time must not exceed their financial ability, or they will have endless trouble in the months to come.

Monkeys will be quite fortunate in their love affairs this month. They will have very good opportunities to meet attractive others, but they should not let their passion get out of their control, or they will surely get burned.

The Tenth Month (7 November – 6 December)

Genius is the infinite capacity for taking pains

This is one of the most unfavourable months of the year for Monkeys. They will be under continuous stress from both their personal and business lives during this period. How to overcome their sorrows and pain will be the major concern of the month. Absorbing these blows quickly will be the best remedy. Otherwise, they may end up suffering a nervous breakdown. The sooner they get over their sorrows, the sooner they will get back on the right track. In fact, this would be a suitable time for Monkeys to go on vacation.

Monkeys may face financial problems during this period. Although they will have a steady income, there will be many unexpected expenses which will prove too much for them if they haven't saved up enough in previous months.

Monkeys will be quite weak physically this month. However, their major concern is not about their health, but their road safety. They should walk and drive with extreme care during this period of time.

The Eleventh Month (7 December – 4 January)

Do right and fear no man

The fortune of Monkeys will be much improved this month, so they should try to make use of this period to carry out their projects. They would have a much better chance of success because of the appearance of several Lucky Stars within their Sign. As long as they are doing their job properly without breaking any regulations or laws, Monkeys should not care too much about what other people get up to. There will be several irrational complaints and objections raised this month, yet Monkeys should take little notice of these, or their work will suffer unnecessary delay. Monkeys should keep in mind that self-determination and self-confidence will be the two essential factors in their success during this period of time.

Monkeys will be able to enjoy a sweet and romantic period with their lovers. They will receive a nice surprise if they have the guts to ask for a date, or to make a proposal.

The health of Monkeys will be in much better shape this month, but they should try not to over-indulge in sex and drugs. They should not hesitate to receive proper medical treatments if anything goes wrong with their health.

The Twelfth Month (5 January – 3 February)

Wealth is conspicuous, but poverty hides

Monkeys will be under continuous threat of robbery and burglary this month, so they must try to make sure that all the windows and doors of their houses and offices are secure. Most important of all, Monkeys should try not to show off too much in money affairs. If their valuables or property become too conspicuous, they will surely become the victims of serious crime this month. Apart from this, they should take good care of their wallets and belongings when they are out and about.

It would be much better for Monkeys to be more conservative in handling their expenses, or they will run short of money in the months to come. This month is definitely not a good time for Monkeys to try their luck in gambling or high-risk investments. Monkeys should keep in mind that they should never turn a cold shoulder to those poorer than themselves, or they will land in deep trouble.

Romance will turn over a new leaf this month. A damaged relationship will be much improved. There will probably be a rebirth of a dying love for Monkeys.

Using Feng Shui to Improve Fortune: Directions, Colours, Numbers and Lucky Charm

The ancient Chinese used the traditional Horoscope to predict their fortune on a yearly basis – they used the art of Feng Shui to improve their luck.

It was their belief that the application of tactical Feng Shui would change their bad luck into good, and make their good luck improve even more.

This same method is still effective in today's modern world.

There are four main elements which I will use in tactical Feng Shui:

◆ Lucky Directions
◆ Lucky Colours
◆ Lucky Numbers
◆ Lucky Charm

Although this is not a very successful year for Monkeys, they will enjoy a pretty happy and smooth life with their friends, relatives and colleagues. They should try their best to improve their personal relations if they want to face less opposition at work. Personal disputes will hurt their careers seriously, so they should try to settle these as quickly as possible. Monkeys will have an abundant income coming in steadily. They will be quite healthy in the first part of the year, but the situation will become worse towards year end. Most important of all, they should watch out for their safety when they are on any journeys. Monkeys will enjoy sweet relations with their lovers this year.

I would suggest applying the following Feng Shui tactics to improve luck so that Monkeys don't have to worry too much about their fate within the year.

Lucky Directions

The most favourable directions of the year for the Monkey are **South**, **Southeast** and **North**. Monkeys should sleep or sit in these directions if they wish to improve their fortune.

To make this procedure very simple, divide the house or room into nine imaginary squares. Then, using a compass, check the exact direction of each square as shown in Figure 4. This will help to ensure that you do not make a mistake with the direction.

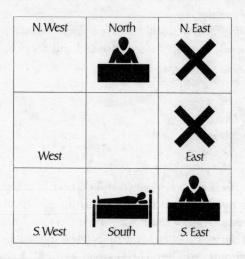

Figure 4

Monkeys should sit in the relevant directions at work or while studying; this will ensure that their achievements are much greater than the Stars intended. To improve health and achieve a good night's sleep, the Monkey should position the bed in the favourable direction shown (South).

However, Monkeys should try to keep away from their unfavourable directions of the year; that is, East and Northeast as shown in Figure 4. The Monkey should try not to sit, work or sleep in these directions, in order to get rid of the negative influences lurking there.

Lucky Colours

According to Chinese tradition, each of the five elements has its own representative colours. Fire is represented by red, pink and purple, Earth by yellow and brown, and so on. As a Feng Shui Master I would suggest **green**, **yellow** and **brown** as the Monkey's lucky colours for the year 2001.

Use these colours in paints, wall coverings, rugs, drapes and curtains. This will be sure to bring them good fortune within the year.

However, the Monkey should try not to use pink, purple or blue in 2001, to avoid bad luck.

Lucky Numbers

The lucky numbers for the Monkey in 2001 are: **2** and **8**.

Fortune will be much improved by using these lucky numbers whenever possible. For example, if the Monkey has a choice, the phone number 228-3388 is better than 356-5256 – because the former contains more twos and eights, the Monkey's two lucky numbers for the year.

Lucky Charm

Feng Shui Masters believe that special objects can be used as a medium between human beings and nature. The fortune of the recipient is greatly improved as the positive wave of energy from nature is passed through the object or 'lucky charm' on to the recipient.

The lucky charm for the Monkey in 2001 is a pair of magpies made of bright yellow stone. This pair of magpies with a Chinese character 'Happiness' inscribed on their chests, one standing on a three-section bamboo, and one standing on a branch with three plums on it, is shown below. For the best result, they should be placed in the north or the southeast direction of the house.

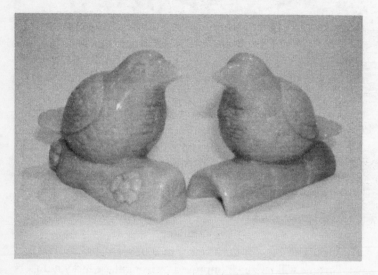

Chapter Five

The

Rooster

Years of the Rooster

1909 (4/Feb/09—3/Feb/10) 1957 (4/Feb/57—3/Feb/57)
1921 (4/Feb/21—3/Feb/22) 1969 (4/Feb/69—3/Feb/70)
1933 (4/Feb/33—3/Feb/34) 1981 (4/Feb/81—3/Feb/82)
1945 (4/Feb/45—3/Feb/46) 1993 (4/Feb/93—3/Feb/94)

Distribution of the Stars within the Sign for 2001

Lucky Stars	Unlucky Stars
The Three Pillars	Flying Spell
The Star of Commander	Legal Spell
Earthly Salvation	Five Ghosts
	Seductive Red

Lucky Stars

The Three Pillars

In ancient China, the *Ding* was a large and heavy cooking pot supported by three strong legs. As the Ding has been used to symbolize the government, the three legs have symbolized the three prime ministers of the government, who worked as the solid support of the whole country. These ministers possessed absolute power to keep everything under control.

The appearance of this Star is a very good omen. It indicates enough confidence and strength to overcome opponents and challengers, and triumph if a person commits him- or herself to a goal.

The Star of Commander

Although the ancient Chinese loved peace, they also respected their local military commander, who was there to protect them from foreign enemies. A courageous and responsible commander signified a guardian of the peace and protection from suffering.

The appearance of this Star is a very good omen. It will not only enrich a Sign's luck, but will also minimize negative influences from Unlucky Stars.

Earthly Salvation

There are three 'Salvation' Stars in the Chinese Horoscope: 'Heavenly Salvation', 'Earthly Salvation' and 'God of Salvation'. They are all considered to have the power to help people out of trouble and disasters. Among the three, 'Earthly Salvation' is the least important. Still, its appearance is a good omen for those in trouble.

When this Star appears, people's suffering will be alleviated. Nonetheless, people should still try to keep themselves out of difficulty, since the Star's influence is not so strong.

Unlucky Stars
Flying Spell

In ancient times, Chinese magic spells were created through special symbols and characters written by Taoist priests in red ink or even blood. Based on this, the concept of five 'Evil Spell' Stars in the Chinese Horoscope developed. This is one of them.

As its name suggests, the Flying Spell was the kind that flew through the sky, invisible to the human eye. When someone experienced bad luck it was blamed on an unfortunate encounter with such a flying spell.

When this Star appears, people should try to keep a low profile and be alert to prepare for unexpected troubles or even accidents.

Legal Spell

This is one of the five 'Magic Spell' Stars in the Chinese Horoscope. The ancient Chinese believed that the family would get entangled in lawsuits as a result of an encounter with this spell.

When this Star appears, people need to watch their conduct and follow the rules. They should be very careful in managing their affairs to avoid legal problems or lawsuits.

Five Ghosts

The Chinese believe that ghosts are best avoided, since they threaten people's health and safety. To living people, meeting five ghosts at once would definitely be a horrible experience. Surely, then, this Star is not a good omen.

The appearance of this Star is a warning to play it safe. Avoid provoking anyone in a position of authority, or it could lead to an endless nightmare.

Seductive Red

Confucianism advised people to try their best to restrain themselves from sexual seduction, or they might lose their way or even collapse. As a result, beauty became almost the equivalent to poison in ancient China. Red and beautiful flowers were avoided in order to keep them from temptation.

The appearance of this Star is an indication of sexual troubles in the coming year. People should keep alert and should not indulge themselves too much.

General Overview of the Year

Roosters will be very successful in their careers this year if they really try their best to do so. Their success will depend on their absolute power to keep everything under control. Roosters will be the big losers if they fail to demonstrate strong leadership to the people around them. Roosters should try to keep away from false friends, or their careers will be damaged seriously. If there are any legal cases arising this year, Roosters should try to settle them as soon as possible.

Financially, Roosters will have a fortunate year in money affairs. They will see satisfactory returns from investments, but they should try to keep this a secret.

Roosters will be quite healthy this year, but they must try to avoid over-eating and over-drinking.

There will be a new romance for Roosters, but it will not prove easy for them to hold on to this relationship.

Career   ★★★
Money   ★★★
Health   ★★
Love   ★

★★★ = Pretty Good/★★ = Fair/★ = Unsatisfactory

Career ***

If they can try to keep things under control, Roosters will be very successful in their careers this year. However, they'll have to fight very hard before they can gain important achievements, because they won't get something for nothing. Roosters will have better opportunities at work during the third, fourth, seventh, eighth, ninth and the last month of the year. They will be more successful if they try to make good use of these months to carry out their business plans. However, Roosters will spoil their opportunities if they fail to show their strong determination and leadership to the people around them. Roosters must try to keep away from false friends or their careers will be damaged seriously. Roosters should try to handle their documents and contracts with extreme care if they don't want to be involved in any lawsuits. Actually, the best way forward is to try to settle any legal cases as soon as possible.

Money ***

This will be a very fortunate year for Roosters. They will have satisfactory returns from investments, but they'll have to keep this under wraps. Their most fortunate financial months of the year will be the third, fourth, seventh, ninth and the last month of the year. However, Roosters should not try their luck at gambling or high-risk investments, or they will lose a lot of money. It would be much better for them to avoid any games of chance during the first two months, the fifth, eighth and tenth month.

Health **

Roosters will be quite healthy this year, so they don't have too much to worry on this front. Their major concern will be their diet. Over-eating and over-drinking will bring endless trouble to them towards the end of the year. The months that they have to pay special attention to their diet will be the first, second, sixth and the last month of the year. Apart from this, Roosters have to watch out for their personal safety during the fourth, fifth, eighth and eleventh month.

Love *

Roosters will be looking for a new romance this year, but may be unsuccessful until year's end. Even then, it will be quite difficult for them to keep hold of this relationship. Roosters will have better opportunities in their love affairs during the fourth, seventh, ninth, eleventh and the last month of the year. It would be much better if Roosters try to be more open-minded and avoid being self-centred in their love affairs. Otherwise, they may face a broken relationship sooner or later within the year.

According to traditional Chinese astrology, the distributions of the Lucky and Unlucky Stars within a Sign will more or less determine a person's fate in a particular year. Just as the distributions of the Stars change from year to year, however, they also change from month to month. Each Sign's fate for the year and for each month is calculated according to this basic rule.

Monthly In-depth Forecasts
The First Month (4 February – 4 March)

A fool and his money are soon parted

Roosters will be easily cheated this month, so they must try to watch out for dirty tricks. Particularly, Roosters should try to watch out for money traps, or they will lose a lot of money. Somebody may try to make use of their sympathy to fool them, so they have to be clever enough not to fall into any traps. This month is definitely not a fortunate period for Roosters to risk their money in gambling or investments. Apart from this, there be will several unexpected expenses for Roosters this month, so they should try to save more.

Roosters should try to handle their business by themselves as much as possible. They will only be deceived if they depend too much on others to do their jobs for them.

Fortunately, Roosters will be quite healthy this month. However, they have to mind their diet and try not to eat or drink too much, particularly at social gatherings.

The Second Month (5 March – 4 April)

Don't put all your eggs in one basket

Roosters will suffer a big loss in money affairs this month because of the appearance of several Unlucky Stars within their Sign. Therefore, they must take good care of their money. They should not put all their eggs in one basket. It would be much better if Roosters could switch investments from one single project to different projects. Apart from this, Roosters should try to keep alert to protect themselves from a robbery or burglary.

Roosters will probably end up with nothing at month's end if they put all their time and effort into a single project. They stand a better chance of success if they engage in several projects at the same time.

It would be much better for Roosters to try to reach a mutual understanding with their lovers during this month. Otherwise, they will face a broken relationship very soon.

The Third Month (5 April – 4 May)

After a storm comes a calm

This is one of the most favourable months of the year for Roosters, so they should try to make good use of this period of time if they want to see some real achievement at year's end. Most of the difficulties and problems that have troubled them over the past two months will disappear this month. Consequently, Roosters can manage their work efficiently this month. They will be more successful if they can demonstrate their outstanding leadership qualities to their fellow-workers. It's time for Roosters to think about future developments.

Money affairs will be much improved and investments will bring satisfactory returns for Roosters this month. However, they should try to keep a low profile and not show off too much because they are still under the threat of a robbery or burglary.

Roosters are eagerly looking for a breakthrough in love this month. Unfortunately they will most likely be disappointed in the face of cruel reality. However, Roosters will be able to find a comfortable and peaceful shelter in their homes.

The Fourth Month (5 May – 4 June)

A rising tide lifts all boats

Business matters will improve somewhat this month. Actually, it's time for a revolutionary change at work, and Roosters will be very successful and productive if they dare to take action now. Roosters had better not hesitate too much in taking action, since time and tide wait for no one. They will be very sorry if they let this rare opportunity slip away. Roosters may get a promotion this month, but they should not forget or avoid their old companions or they will be isolated at work sooner or later.

Roosters will be quite fortunate this month in money affairs. They will see income from different sources. However, they should keep on watching their budget to make sure that their expenses are not getting out of control.

Roosters will be quite healthy this month, but they must watch out for their road safety very carefully at the end of the month. Apart from this, Roosters should try not to go fishing or swimming alone in the morning hours this month.

The Fifth Month (5 June – 6 July)

You can't win them all

Roosters will face certain challenges at work this month. They'll have to put more time and effort in to overcome these challenges if they don't want to suffer an unexpected defeat. However, Roosters should not be too ambitious. Just as the old saying goes, 'You can't win them all.' Roosters should be satisfied with a reasonable compromise with opponents. Apart from this, Roosters should never try to challenge their superiors or get involved in power struggles. They'll end up very sorry very soon should they do so. They should keep in mind that a mild and humble attitude will help them be successful in the coming months.

Roosters have to take good care of their eyes and ears this month. They should go to a doctor for proper medical treatment as soon as possible if anything seems amiss. Any delays will be dangerous and harmful to them.

Roosters should be faithful to their lovers and never cheat on them this month. Otherwise there will be endless trouble in the near future.

The Sixth Month (7 July – 6 August)

Silence is golden

This is one of most unfavourable months of the year for Roosters, so they should try to be more conservative and cautious in handling their daily affairs. Once again, a mild and humble attitude will help them to overcome hardships smoothly. Talking too much will be their major handicap this month, so they should try to keep their mouth shut. It would be much better to say nothing, particularly about their business, nor should they spread any rumours or gossip (especially about superiors). They should keep in mind that 'Silence is golden.'

Money matters will fluctuate from time to time this month. Roosters will be big losers if they risk money in gambling or huge investments. They should wait for a better time. Most important of all, Roosters should not talk too much about their financial affairs, to avoid a robbery or even a kidnapping.

Roosters have to watch out for unhealthy foreign foods when they travel abroad. They should also make sure they get any necessary injections before their journey.

The Seventh Month (7 August – 6 September)

Opportunity doesn't knock twice

There will be several business opportunities knocking at the door during this period. Roosters will miss a good opportunity for major success if they fail to answer in time. They won't get a second chance. Perhaps someone offers them a role in a joint business or investment venture. Roosters should consider this offer carefully even if at first it does not seem very attractive or worthwhile. This month is a very good time for Roosters to carry out new projects or start a business. However, Roosters must turn down all offers related to illegal activities, or they will be in deep trouble in the months to come.

This is a profitable month for Roosters. Besides their steady usual income, Roosters will have luck in lottery and gambling. However, they should not be too greedy because their fortune will turn bad towards the end of the month.

It's not a good time for Roosters to take a vacation abroad. If they must travel, they have to watch their money and safety carefully.

The Eighth Month (7 September – 7 October)

The sooner begun, the sooner done

Hesitation will be the major hurdle to success this month. As the old saying goes, 'the sooner begun, the sooner done.' Roosters will be able to complete their tasks on time if they don't waste time hesitating. Having said this, Roosters should try to find the proper partners at work and enlist their aid. Choosing the incorrect partners will seriously hurt their careers later on.

There will not be too much wrong health-wise this month. The main health concern this month surrounds children. Roosters must never leave children home alone during this period. Roosters should also keep an eye out for fire at the office.

Roosters must not cheat on their lovers; honesty is the best policy in dealing with their lovers during this period.

The Ninth Month (8 October – 6 November)

Strike while the iron is hot

Now's the best time for Roosters to take action regarding future development, because they are reaching the peak of their fortune. Just the old saying goes, 'Strike while the iron is hot.' Roosters should try to make good use of this good time for growing their business. Apart from this, Roosters should try to bargain for more benefits for themselves since their bargaining power is very strong this month. Roosters have to try to be punctual for business appointments and meetings, or they will miss out on several opportunities.

This is a profitable month for Roosters. They'll receive quite a good income from investments. It's also a good time to start up new investments.

Roosters have a very good chance of meeting their dream-lover during this period. However, it will be difficult for them to maintain this very delicate relationship. They should hope for the best and prepare for the worst.

are best

...ne of Roosters will suddenly drop sharply this month. ...lties and disputes will come up as suddenly as thunder-...rms. Consequently it's necessary for Roosters to handle their work with caution, or they will suffer deeply from a sudden big fall in careers. They must try to keep themselves calm enough to have second thoughts, because any hasty decisions during this period will lead them to the road of destruction. Apart from this, Roosters should keep in mind that they should never try to challenge or provoke people in authority, or there will be endless trouble in the months to come.

Roosters should not turn a cold shoulder to their new or old friends, and especially not to their lovers. If they do, they will surely be ostracized later on. Roosters should try not to be self-centred or arrogant in social affairs this month.

It would be much better for Roosters to have second thoughts regarding expenses and investments within this unfortunate period, because it will keep them from losing a lot of money and will help them to avoid falling into money traps.

The Eleventh Month (7 December – 4 January)

Love and desire are the spirit's wings to great deeds

Roosters have to fight very hard for career success this month. They will be left far behind by their opponents if they lose concentration at work. Lack of determination will be the major limitation this month, so Roosters should try to stay focused. Their kindness and generosity to the people around them will make them popular and successful right now.

This will be a romantic month for Roosters. Their love and desire will bring a lot of joy – not only to them, but also to their friends. However, they should try not to let their love affair mixed up with their work, or both will be spoiled.

Health will be much improved, but Roosters must watch out for their road safety. They must walk and drive carefully, particularly at night, this month.

The Twelfth Month (5 January – 3 February)

Diligence is the mother of good fortune

Although the fortune of Roosters will be much improved this month, they'll have to work very hard for their success. They should keep in mind that diligence will bring good fortune to them and nothing can be achieved without their sweat. Other than diligence, caution is also very important to their success during this period, so Roosters should handle their documents and contracts with extreme care if they don't want to get involved in lawsuits. If possible, Roosters should try to settle disputes and legal cases as soon as possible by any means necessary.

Roosters will have some luck in lottery and gambling this month because of the appearance of several Lucky Stars within their Sign. However, they should try to check whether there are any flaws in their accounts. Otherwise, their hard-earned money will be swallowed up by some other people sooner or later.

Roosters will have a very good chance of finding true love at the end of the month. They should try to keep a low profile and keep this new love a secret, or some jealous people may try to spoil it.

ncient Chinese used the traditional Horoscope to predict their fortune on a yearly basis – they used the art of Feng Shui to improve their luck.

It was their belief that the application of tactical Feng Shui would change their bad luck into good, and make their good luck improve even more.

This same method is still effective in today's modern world.

There are four main elements which I will use in tactical Feng Shui:

- ◆ Lucky Directions
- ◆ Lucky Colours
- ◆ Lucky Numbers
- ◆ Lucky Charm

Roosters will be very successful in career matters this year if they really try their best to do so. They should try to keep away from false friends. They should handle contracts and legal documents with extreme care if they don't want to be involved in lawsuits. This will be a fortunate year for Roosters in money affairs. They will see satisfactory returns from their investments. Although Roosters will be quite healthy this year, they should try to keep away from raw or unhygienic foods, especially during the first three months of the year. Roosters will turn a new page in their love affairs at year end, but they have to pay special attention to take care of this very delicate relationship.

I would suggest applying the following Feng Shui tactics to ensure greater success throughout the year.

Lucky Directions

The most favourable directions of the year for Roosters are **Southeast**, **North** and **Northeast**. Roosters should sleep or sit in these directions if they wish to improve their fortune.

To make this procedure very simple, divide the house or room into nine imaginary squares. Then, using a compass, check the exact direction of each square as shown in Figure 5. This will help to ensure that you do not make a mistake with the direction.

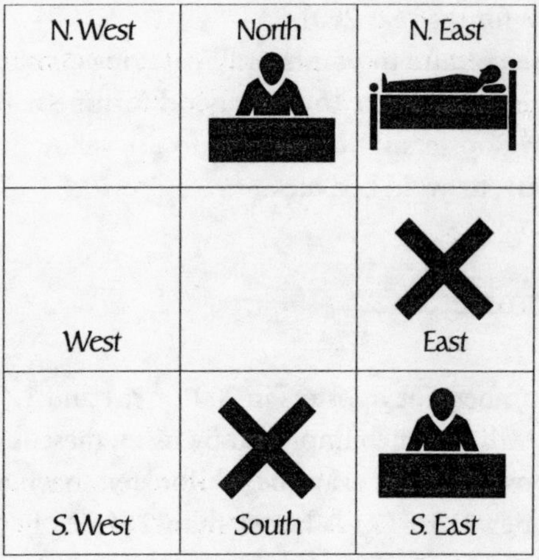

Figure 5

The Rooster should sit in the relevant directions at work or while studying; this will ensure that their achievements are much greater than the Stars intended. To improve health and achieve a good night's sleep, Roosters should position their bed in the favourable direction shown (Northeast).

However, Roosters should try to keep away from the unfavourable directions of the year; that is, East and South as shown in Figure 5. The Rooster should try not to sit, work or sleep

ıours

According to Chinese tradition, each of the five elements has its own representative colours. Fire is represented by red, pink and purple, Earth by yellow and brown, and so on. As a Feng Shui Master I would suggest **blue**, **grey**, **black** and **white** as Roosters's lucky colours for the year 2001.

Use these colours in paints, wall coverings, rugs, drapes and curtains. This will be sure to bring good fortune within the year.

However, Roosters should try not to use yellow, brown, red or purple in 2001, to avoid bad luck.

Lucky Numbers

The lucky numbers for Roosters in 2001 are: **1** and **3**.

Fortune will be much improved by using these lucky numbers whenever possible. For example, if Roosters have a choice, the phone number 213-3123 is better than 244-4834 – because the former contains more ones and threes, Roosters's two lucky numbers of the year.

Lucky Charm

Feng Shui Masters believe that special objects can be used as a medium between human beings and nature. The fortune of the recipient is greatly improved as the positive wave of energy from nature is passed through the object or 'lucky charm' on to the recipient.

The lucky charm for the Rooster in 2001 is a white st
ing with a dragon and a carp playing with a pearl in water,
shown below. For the best result, this stone carving should be
placed in the northeast or the southeast direction of the house.

Chapter Six

狗

The

Dog

Years of the Dog

1910 (4/Feb/10—4/Feb/11)   1958 (4/Feb/58—3/Feb/59)
1922 (4/Feb/22—4/Feb/23)   1970 (4 Feb/70—3 Feb/71)
1934 (4/Feb/34—4/Feb/35)   1982 (4 Feb/82—3 Feb/83)
1946 (4/Feb/46—3/Feb/47)   1994 (4 Feb/94—3 Feb/95)

Distribution of the Stars within the Sign for 2001

Lucky Stars   Unlucky Stars

Red Phoenix   Deadly Spell
Lunar Virtue   Gradual Drain
Commander's Saddle

Lucky Stars

Red Phoenix

In traditional Chinese culture the phoenix was a legendary, mystical bird, famous for spending time in romantic, affectionate pairs. Over time it came to symbolize love and marriage, and for centuries it has been included in Chinese wedding ceremonies.

The appearance of this Star is a very good omen. It indicates a romantic year with good marriage possibilities.

Lunar Virtue

Virtue was highly appreciated by Confucius. The ancient Chinese believed that virtue not only set a good example for others to follow, but also produced its own rewards. Lunar Virtue is the least important of the four 'Virtue' Stars in the Chinese Horoscope, but is especially favourable for women.

When this Star appears, people will have enhanced persuasive skills which can help them achieve important breakthroughs. The effectiveness of this Star is usually not strong enough to suppress the Unlucky Stars if there are too many of them appearing together within a Sign.

Commander's Saddle

In ancient China, military commanders fought their battles on horseback. In battle a good saddle was essential for brave and effective fighting. As a result, the idea of a commander's saddle came to symbolize courage and military superiority.

Should this Star appear within the Sign, people can conquer life's obstacles if they are courageous enough. However, remember to be merciful towards defeated enemies.

Unlucky Stars

Deadly Spell

In ancient times, Chinese magic spells were created through special symbols and characters written by Taoist priests in red ink or

..nis, the concept of five 'Magic Spell' Stars in
.ope developed.

.rious Star of all is the 'Deadly Spell'. The ancient
.ved that shortly before a person's death the Ruler of
.d send an invisible 'Deadly Spell' as a summons to the
.e.

When this Star appears, people have to be very careful about
their health and safety, to avoid serious illness, injury or even death.

Gradual Drain

Farming has been the major source of income for Chinese peasants for centuries. Because water is essential for irrigation, it has
come to symbolize wealth. Over the centuries, Chinese peasants
have worked to prevent drainage from their cultivated lands.

Similarly, when this Star appears people need to watch their
expenditure and keep within their budget. They should also avoid
risky investments and gambling, which could easily lead to financial ruin.

General Overview of the Year

Dogs can expect to have a very fortunate and romantic year ahead.
However, they have to put more time and effort in at work if they
want to be more successful. Their positive and aggressive attitude
will bring splendid achievements. Dogs will be able to win the
whole-hearted support of subordinates and partners if they show
due care and consideration to them from time to time. Over-
expansion and over-expenditure will be the two main threats to
their success in business this year.

Financially, this will be a fortunate year for Dogs. But they
should not let their greediness blind them or lead them to total
destruction.

Health will be quite unstable this year. Dogs should watch their
diet and personal hygiene closely in order to avoid infection. Apart
from this, they should try not to get too close to water.

This will be a very romantic year for Dogs, and a happy marriage can be expected within the year.

Career ****
Money **
Health *
Love ***

**** = Very Fortunate/*** = Pretty Good/** = Fair/* = Unsatisfactory

Career ****

Dogs would be quite productive this year if they wish to put extra time and effort in at work. However, they would be even more successful if they keep a positive and aggressive attitude while carrying out their work throughout the year. Generally speaking, Dogs will have better opportunities at work during the first, fifth and the last two months of the year. Dogs should show their care and consideration to fellow-workers constantly if they want to have their whole-hearted support, which will prove crucial to Dogs' success. However, Dogs will face problems during the second, third, seventh and eighth month of the year. Dogs must keep an eye on their budget throughout the year, because over-expansion and over-expenditure will be the two main threats to their business success this year. In other words, Dogs should try to keep their budget under control.

Money **

Financially, this will be a fortunate year for Dogs. They will have luck in lottery and gambling occasionally throughout the year, but they should not let their greediness lead them to destruction. Dogs will have better luck in money affairs during the first, fifth and

Health will fluctuate from time to time throughout the year. Dogs should watch their diets closely to avoid any infection, which if left unchecked will probably have serious consequences. Dogs should try to take care of themselves particularly during the second, third, fourth and the last month. Apart from this, Dogs must try to keep away from cliffs during the fourth month, and try to watch their home safety during the sixth month. It's much better to be safe than sorry. Moreover, Dogs will suffer from toothache or sore throat during the first and eighth month if they fail to look after their oral hygiene.

Love ***

Although this will be a romantic year for Dogs, they will be confused by their ever-changing situation. They are rich in sentimental attachments. Generally speaking, Dogs will have better luck in their love affairs during the first, fifth and the eleventh month. This year would be a good time for Dogs to get married, especially at the beginning and the end of the year. They will enjoy a sweet family life not only during this year, but also for many years to come.

According to traditional Chinese astrology, the distributions of the Lucky and Unlucky Stars within a Sign will more or less determine a person's fate in a particular year. Just as the distributions of the Stars change from year to year, however, they also change from month to month. Each Sign's fate for the year and for each month is calculated according to this basic rule.

Monthly In-depth Forecasts
The First Month (4 February – 4 March)

Things are beautiful if you love them

Dogs will be in high spirits during this period. Their pleasant manner will lighten the hearts of those around them, and it will be quite possible for Dogs to have a new sweet romance this month. However, they must be courageous enough to express their affection, or opportunities will slip through their fingers. This month would be a very good time for Dogs to take a vacation abroad; they'll be left afterwards with some unforgettable memories.

Dogs will be able to handle their work without too much difficulty during this period. However, they should try their best to improve their personal and business relationships if they wish to be more successful in the following months. Dogs will be able to reach a very important business agreement as they are most persuasive right now.

This month will be very fortunate financially for Dogs. Apart from their abundant income, Dogs will have luck in lottery and gambling. But they should not be too greedy.

The Second Month (5 March – 4 April)

Don't count your chickens before they're hatched

Although Dogs will be quite productive at work this month, they should not be too optimistic about future development and should not risk over-expansion. There will probably be a drop in sales in the coming two months, so Dogs should try to be more conservative and cautious in business. It's time for Dogs to reconsider future development if they want to have a successful year.

Financially, Dogs should not count their chickens before they are hatched, because something unexpected might happen. Dogs must watch their budget carefully to avoid over-expenditure this month.

...ıore time with family this month. The
...elease them from the stresses of workaday
...y what they need this month.

...d Month (5 April – 4 May)

One ...ad apple spoils the whole barrel

This is one of the most unfavourable months of the year for Dogs, so they should try to handle their day-to-day work with extreme care. This is definitely not a suitable time for them to take action on new projects, as they will face numerous oppositions and challenges right from the start. Most important of all, Dogs must try to find out who will most endanger the whole business, and then try to get rid of these people as soon as possible. Otherwise, their business will be spoiled sooner or later.

Fortune in money affairs of Dogs will drop to its lowest level. Consequently, Dogs must not try their luck in gambling or high-risk investments, or they will be big losers. Apart from this, it would not be wise for Dogs to buy luxuries or property this month. Even if they really would like to do so, they'll have to wait a few months.

Dogs have to try their best to keep away from false friends. They should keep in mind that they must not let one bad apple spoil the whole barrel.

The Fourth Month (5 May – 4 June)

Health is wealth

Although the fortune of Dogs will be improved a little bit this month, they should keep alert to possible trouble at work. Their major concern this month is their health. Dogs will be very weak physically and mentally. They need to get enough rest and sleep. Success isn't worth it if it means sacrificing one's health. Apart from this, Dogs should not venture near the edge of the cliffs or other high places.

Dogs have to try to release themselves from their heavy workload. It would be much better if they can find others to share their problems and burdens. Dogs should not be too reluctant to ask for assistance from those who really care about them.

Money affairs will come good in the latter part of the month. Consequently, Dogs should not worry too much about money this month.

The Fifth Month (5 June – 6 July)

Fortune favours the brave

Fortune improves this month and will continue to do so over the next two months. Dogs should try to make good use of this period of time if they want to be successful and productive. But, first of all, Dogs must try to bolster their determination and build up their confidence in business. They should not be afraid to take calculated risks at work, or they will miss out on a lot of opportunities this month. Just as the old saying goes, 'Fortune favours the brave.' A positive and aggressive attitude will bring splendid achievements.

The same thing applies in love. Dogs won't get a second chance to show their affection to new acquaintances or lovers.

This would be a very good time for Dogs to make investments. They will see quite good returns in the near future. However, they should try not to let their greediness blind them or lead them to a sudden economic collapse.

The Sixth Month (7 July – 6 August)

Moderation in all things

Dogs will be able to release themselves from the burden of their heavy workload this month. It's a good time for them to take a vacation. They will be much refreshed, both physically and mentally, when they return. The major concern this month is to try to be moderate in all things, to avoid unnecessary trouble. Dogs should keep in mind that extremes will bring nothing but serious damage. On the other hand, understanding and forgiveness will be Dogs' two important keys to future success.

Dogs should not be too aggressive in love affairs this month, or they will scare their lovers away. Nor should they play with fire this month, or they will get burned.

Dogs have to watch their home safety carefully this month. Never leave children alone at home. Try to keep knives and fire far away out of reach of small children.

The Seventh Month (7 August – 6 September)

Old habits die hard

Dogs have to struggle very hard for career survival because of the appearance of several Unlucky Stars within their Sign this month. It's necessary for Dogs to make some changes at this stage, or they will be thrown out of business eventually. Their major concern this month has to do with eliminating bad habits at work. Lack of concentration and consistency, these two old habits of Dogs, should be corrected as soon as possible. Dogs must try their best to eradicate these flaws, or they will be defeated badly.

Dogs must firmly refuse the temptations of drugs this month. They will be on the way to total destruction if they fail to do so.

Dogs should try to give up their extravagant tastes and habits this month. If successful, this would be a big boon to their financial status.

The Eighth Month (7 September – 7 October)

If you want something done well, do it yourself

This is one of the most favourable months of the year for Dogs because of the appearance of several Lucky Stars within their Sign. They will be quite productive at work if they can maintain concentration without too many interruptions. They will be fully supported by their subordinates and fellow-workers this month. However, Dogs should try to handle their business by themselves as much as possible. Just as the old saying goes, 'If you want something done well, do it yourself.' Dogs should therefore not rely too much on other people in this regard.

Dogs should try to check their accounts by themselves. If they find any flaws, it would be much better if Dogs can try to repair them themselves.

Dogs will be in tip-top condition physically. Having said this, they should try to keep their teeth and mouth really clean, or they will suffer very much.

The Ninth Month (8 October – 6 November)

A live dog is better than a dead lion

Difficulties and dangers will come up suddenly as thunderstorms this month, so that Dogs will have to pay special attention to their career and personal safety. Dogs will face severe challenges from their opponents, and strong objections from their colleagues, and these will drive them crazy if they can't handle them properly and promptly. Under these circumstances, Dogs must keep calm and fight hard for their survival. In other words, survival will be the major concern of Dogs this month.

Dogs must stop fooling around with their money. It's definitely not a good time for them to start a new venture. Over-expenditure will be another major concern this month.

Dogs will tend to suffer from injuries this month. Therefore, they should try to keep away from dangerous places and never try to risk their lives this month. They should keep in mind that it is much better to be a live dog than a dead lion.

The Tenth Month (7 November – 6 December)

Cheats never prosper

Although the difficulties and dangers of last month will gradually disappear over the course of this month, Dogs should still be cautious in handling their work and taking care of themselves. Dogs should stop fooling around at work, because they are not fooling anyone else but themselves. Their dirty tricks will never make them prosper. They would be more successful if they were honest to the people around them. They should keep in mind that honesty really is the best policy.

Dogs should also try to be honest to their lovers this month. They will be faced with a very serious situation if they try to cheat on them. Mutual understanding is very important if Dogs wish to keep the relationship running smoothly, without too many quarrels.

Dogs have to keep their eyes wide open for money traps, or they will lose a lot of money – probably much more than they ever anticipated.

The Eleventh Month (7 December – 4 January)

Man creates his own happiness

This is one of the most fortunate months of the year for Dogs, so they should try to make good use of this period of time. Success or failure will be in their own hands. They might end up empty-handed if they are not eager enough to fight for their success. If that happens, they have no one to blame but themselves. Dogs should keep in mind that the more time and effort they put into their business, the more successful they will be. Their efforts this month will never be wasted.

Dogs will have to make a very important decision in their financial affairs. They should try to ask the advice of experts whenever needed, and they shouldn't be blinded by greed or ignorance when it comes to investments this month.

Dogs can look forward to a proposal in love this month. It would be a proper time for them to get married because of the appearance of several Lucky Stars within their Sign. A marriage this month will herald a sweet family life for many years to come.

The Twelfth Month (5 January – 3 February)

Thrift is a great revenue

Although there will be some personal disputes arising this month, yet, it's still quite a fortunate time for Dogs. They will be able to handle their daily work without too much difficulty because they will get the necessary support from subordinates and fellow-workers. But, no matter how successful they are, Dogs should watch their budget when planning future development. Over-expansion will bring only a sudden collapse in the near future. Their major concern this month is not how to earn money, but how to control the outflow of their money. Dogs should keep in mind that thrift is a great revenue.

Extravagance will lead to money problems this month. A tight budget will help Dogs stay out of trouble. They should never get involved with any loans this month.

Health will fluctuate this month. Dogs should watch their diet to avoid any infection, which would bring about serious health consequences immediately.

Using Feng Shui to Improve Fortune: Directions, Colours, Numbers and Lucky Charm

The ancient Chinese used the traditional Horoscope to predict their fortune on a yearly basis – they used the art of Feng Shui to improve their luck.

It was their belief that the application of tactical Feng Shui would change their bad luck into good, and make their good luck improve even more.

This same method is still effective in today's modern world.

There are four main elements which I will use in tactical Feng Shui:

- ◆ Lucky Directions
- ◆ Lucky Colours
- ◆ Lucky Numbers
- ◆ Lucky Charm

Dogs can expect to have a very fortunate and romantic year ahead. Their positive and aggressive attitude will bring splendid achievements. They should show consideration and care to their subordinates and colleagues if they want to gain their full support, which will prove crucial to their success. However, Dogs should try to keep their budget under control if they want to have a productive year. They should not let their greediness lead them to a sudden economic collapse. Health will fluctuate from time to time throughout the year. Dogs have to mind their diets and try to keep away from water, especially during summer time. Although this will be a romantic year for Dogs, yet they will be confused by their ever-changing romance.

I would suggest applying the following Feng Shui tactics to ensure greater success throughout the year.

Lucky Directions

The most favourable directions of the year for the Dog are **East**, **South** and **Northeast**. Dogs should sleep or sit in these directions if they wish to improve their fortune.

To make this procedure very simple, divide the house or room into nine imaginary squares. Then, using a compass, check the exact direction of each square as shown in Figure 6. This will help to ensure that you do not make a mistake with the direction.

N. West	North	N. East
	✗	🛏
West		East
S. West	South	S. East

Figure 6

The Dog should sit in the relevant directions at work or while studying; this will ensure that their achievements are much greater than the Stars intended. To improve health and achieve a good night's sleep, the Dog should position the bed in the favourable direction shown (Northeast).

However, the Dog should try to keep away from the un-favourable directions of the year; that is, Southeast and North as shown in Figure 6. The Dog should try not to sit, work or sleep in these directions, in order to get rid of the negative influences lurking there.

Lucky Colours

According to Chinese tradition, each of the five elements has its own representative colours. Fire is represented by red, pink and purple, Earth by yellow and brown, and so on. As a Feng Shui Master I would suggest **red**, **pink**, **purple**, **yellow** and **brown** as the Dog's lucky colours for the year 2001.

Use these colours in paints, wall coverings, rugs, drapes and curtains. This will be sure to bring good fortune within the year.

However, the Dog should try not to use green or white in 2001 to avoid bad luck.

Lucky Numbers

The lucky numbers for the Dog in 2001 are: **4** and **9**.

Fortune will be much improved by using these lucky numbers whenever possible. For example, if the Dog has a choice, the phone number 249-4294 is better than 265-5457 – because the former contains more fours and nines, the Dog's two lucky numbers for the year.

Lucky Charm

Feng Shui Masters believe that special objects can be used as a medium between human beings and nature. The fortune of the recipient is greatly improved as the positive wave of energy from nature is passed through the object or 'lucky charm' on to the recipient.

The lucky charm for the Dog in 2001 is a pair of elephants stepping on stones with Chinese characters on them saying, 'Everything is refreshing' and 'Good luck as you wish'. There's a pearl at the tip of their raised trunks, as shown below. For the best result, they should be placed in the east or the south direction of the house.

Chapter Seven

The

Pig

Years of the Pig

1911 (5/Feb/11—4/Feb/12)   1959 (4/Feb/59—4/Feb/60)
1923 (5/Feb/23—4/Feb/24)   1971 (4/Feb/71—4/Feb/72)
1935 (5/Feb/35—4/Feb/36)   1983 (4/Feb/83—3/Feb/84)
1947 (4/Feb/47—4/Feb/48)   1995 (4/Feb/95—3/Feb/96)

Distribution of the Stars within the Sign for 2001

Lucky Star	Unlucky Stars
Travelling Horses	Broken Down
	Conflict of the Year
	Iron Bars
	Huge Drain

Lucky Star
Travelling Horses

In ancient China, travelling on horseback was the fastest and easiest way to get around. So, not surprisingly, the horse came to symbolize travel. Whether the journey would be smooth or not depended on the quality and condition of the horse.

When this Star appears it indicates that it is a good year to travel for both business and pleasure.

Unlucky Stars
Broken Down

The ancient Chinese had little regard for objects that were not whole and/or contained cracks. In a similar way, a broken soul was much depreciated.

The appearance of this Star is a bad omen. People should watch out for their morals and conduct. At the same time, they should also try very hard to protect themselves from injury.

Conflict of the Year

Since the ancient Chinese valued harmony, they would try to minimize conflicts quickly, as soon as they broke out. Because this Star signifies conflict, it is not regarded as a good omen.

If this Star appears within a Sign, people have to try their best to settle all disputes and conflicts before they get out of hand. Otherwise they will face a lot of problems and their work will be handicapped as a result.

Iron Bars

In the Chinese Horoscope the Stars 'Iron Bars' and 'Gaol House' are similar to each other in that they both deal with confinement and punishment for a crime. However, 'Iron Bars' is not as serious as 'Gaol House', since the former refers to a place of temporary detention while the latter is more like a maximum-security prison.

When this Star appears, be careful not to break the law – or be prepared to suffer the consequences.

Huge Drain

The ancient Chinese considered water to be the symbol of wealth, since it was essential to agriculture, the backbone of their economy. On a farm, a failure to manage water could easily lead to dried-out crops, spelling disaster.

This Star's appearance is a warning that a large and sudden financial loss is on the horizon.

General Overview of the Year

This will not be a very good year for Pigs in either career or money matters, so they must be very conservative in handling these things. Pigs must try to change their old attitudes and systems at work if they want to survive. They will see much better progress if they go to work in foreign lands. It's very important for Pigs to keep away from anything illegal this year, or they will be in deep trouble and end up in gaol.

This won't be a profitable year for Pigs, so they must try to save for the rainy days ahead.

Their health will not be so good, so it is necessary for Pigs to cut out their bad habits such as heavy smoking and drinking.

This is definitely not a romantic year for Pigs. They will be deeply disappointed if they are seeking new love this year.

Career   *
Money   *
Health   * *
Love   *

* * = Fair/ * = Unsatisfactory

Career *

Pigs will face numerous problems and conflicts at work this year, so they should be more cautious and conservative in handling their business or they will be badly defeated by their opponents. Pigs must try to change their usual attitudes and working systems if they want to be able to overcome the difficulties they face. Otherwise, it will be quite difficult for them to survive in business. However, there will be a much better chance for them if they wish to start up a business in a foreign country. The favourable months for business will be on the second, fifth, sixth and tenth; Pigs should try to make good use of these months if they don't want to end up with nothing at the end of the year.

Pigs have to improve their personal relations with those around them, or their opportunities for success will be diminished. Most important of all, Pigs must try to cut any illegal connections, if any exist, or they will surely end up behind bars.

Money *

This will not be a fortunate year for Pigs in money matters, so they should not try their luck in gambling. They must also be very conservative about handling their investments throughout the year. However, the major concern for Pigs this year is to watch their budget and expenses, or there will be a large and sudden financial loss. Pigs should pay special attention to their money affairs during the first two months, the sixth and also the last two months of the year. It's necessary for Pigs to save more money for rainy days within the year.

Health **

The health of Pigs will not be as good as last year, so they should try to cut out bad habits such as heavy smoking and drinking. Most important of all, Pigs must never try drugs if they don't want to become helpless victims. The months that Pigs should pay special attention to their health and safety will be the fourth, fifth and the eighth month. Apart from this, Pigs should also take good care of the health and safety of their children at home during the second and seventh month.

Love *

This is definitely not a romantic year for Pigs. They will be deeply disappointed if they are looking for a new true love this year. Having said this, Pigs will have better luck in their love affairs during the first, sixth and tenth month. One thing Pigs have to keep in mind is that they should not play with fire and cheat on their lovers, or they will get burned this year.

According to traditional Chinese astrology, the distributions of the Lucky and Unlucky Stars within a Sign will more or less determine a person's fate in a particular year. Just as the distributions of the Stars change from year to year, however, they also change from month to month. Each Sign's fate for the year and for each month is calculated according to this basic rule.

Monthly In-depth Forecasts
The First Month (4 February – 4 March)

Do unto others as you would have them do unto you

There will be several personal disputes within this period; Pigs should try to settle them as soon as possible, or they will bring about endless trouble in the months to come. The major concern of the month for Pigs is their personal relationships – they must improve these by showing proper respect for others. By being more considerate to the people around them, Pigs will not find themselves isolated at work. 'Do unto others as you would have them do unto you.' Pigs should always keep this old saying in mind this month. Pigs will face less opposition if they are willing to compromise rather than confront this month.

Money affairs will fluctuate this month, so it would be much better if Pigs stop trying their luck in gambling and high-risk investments. Otherwise they might lose more money than they ever anticipated.

Fortunately, Pigs will have pretty good luck in love this month. They will be quite popular and they will have a sweet and romantic time with their lovers during this period.

The Second Month (5 March – 4 April)

Well begun is half done

Fortune will be much improved this month because of the appearance of several Lucky Stars within the Sign. Therefore, Pigs should try to take quick action if they want to be successful in future business development. A solid plan plus efficient action will ensure a good start for Pigs at work. Pigs could waste a very good opportunity if they don't start things right. Hesitation and inefficiency will be the two major handicaps for the success of Pigs; they should therefore try to do something to overcome these hurdles.

Pigs seem to be quite fortunate at the beginning of the month. However, their luck will drop down sharply near month's end, so they should try to be more conservative in expenses and investments. They should try to save more money for the rainy days to come in the months ahead.

Health will be quite good this month, but Pigs have to watch their home safety in the latter part of the month. They should pay special attention to the health and safety of children at home, and they must make sure that they receive proper care if anything happens unexpectedly.

The Third Month (5 April – 4 May)

The unexpected always happens

This is one of the most unfavourable months of the year for Pigs, so they should keep alert to possible difficulties and try to sort them out at the earliest possible time. However, the unexpected always happens. Therefore, Pigs should try to equip themselves psychologically to prepare for the worst, so they won't lose their head even in an emergency. This is definitely not a good time for Pigs to start any new projects or new business ventures. In addition, Pigs should try to keep a low profile in order to avoid attacks from jealous people around them at the office.

Money affairs will be like a roller-coaster this month. Pigs should try their best to pay all their bills as soon as possible. In addition, Pigs must watch their wallets and valuable items carefully to avoid theft or burglary.

Pigs should never ignore their lovers this month, or they will be very sorry about that very soon. They risk turning their lovers into strangers.

The Fourth Month (5 May – 4 June)

A stitch in time saves nine

There will be numerous difficulties and challenges at work this month, and they will be quite difficult to handle. Pigs have to put extra attention and effort into settling these before things get out of control. Just as the old saying goes, 'A stitch in time saves nine.' Pigs should try to take remedial measures before the situation gets worse and worse. It's very important for Pigs to keep away from any illegal activity, or they will be punished this month.

Pigs will be quite weak physically, and will tend to suffer from infections this month. Therefore, they have to take good care of themselves and must go to see a doctor for proper medical treatment as soon as something seems amiss with their health.

Their love relationships will be at a serious stage this month. Unless Pigs try to remedy the situation, they will face a broken relationship much sooner than they ever anticipated.

The Fifth Month (5 June – 6 July)

Travel broadens the mind

Gradually, the difficulties and challenges will fade away this month, so that Pigs will be released from the heavy burdens of last month. This month would be a very good time for Pigs to take a vacation, because this will not only refresh them but will also broaden their mind. The information they pick up while travelling will prove very useful for future development. Apart from this, Pigs will meet someone very attractive on their journeys, but they should not expect too much because this new romance will only be short-lived.

Although health is improving this month, Pigs should try to cut out their old bad habits such as heavy smoking and drinking. In addition, Pigs should try to avoid dangerous places such as cliffs and high walls.

This will be one of the most fortunate months in money affairs for Pigs this year. They will have luck in lottery and gambling, but they should try to cut out their extravagant habits or they will end up with nothing by month's end.

The Sixth Month (7 July – 6 August)

If the shoe fits, wear it

Pigs will become quite creative and capable this month, so it would be a very good time for them to carry out new projects. They will have a very good chance of success should they do so. Pigs should try to open themselves up to different ideas if they want to be more successful in their careers. Just as the old saying goes, 'If the shoe fits, wear it' – Pigs shouldn't restrict themselves too much when it comes to choosing projects and investments. Most important of all, Pigs should try to give up their old attitudes and procedures, and renovate their business. Their refusal to do so will bring nothing to them but a total collapse sooner or later.

Pigs will tend to be blinded by prejudice in money affairs this month. It would be much better if they would ask the advice of financial consultants before they make any decisions regarding buying property or making investments.

Pigs should not be too picky with their friends and lovers this month, or they will be left isolated. Pigs should keep in mind that their friendships will bring them joy and admiration, much more than they ever expected.

The Seventh Month (7 August – 6 September)

No pain, no gain

Pigs will have to fight very hard for their career this month, or they will be badly defeated. They must stand firm because they can't afford to lose any ground at work this month. Their extra effort and anguish will prove worthwhile. They will gain nothing this month without any sacrifice. Apart from this, Pigs should try not to challenge or criticize their superiors, lest they be burdened with an extra heavy workload which will prove too much for them.

Although money matters will be quite good at the beginning

of the month, Pigs must save more money for the rainy days to come at the end of the year.

There will be problems about the safety of children at home this month. Pigs should keep alert and watch out for possible dangers such as sharp knives, broken glass, etc.

The Eighth Month (7 September – 7 October)

Hasty climbers have sudden falls

This is one of the most unfortunate months of the year for Pigs, so they should be more cautions and conservative in handling their business to prevent a sudden collapse this month. They should keep in mind that there won't be any short-cuts for them; they have to go step by step in performing their duties. Any decision or action taken in haste will come a cropper. Apart from this, Pigs should try to keep their words or they will lose the necessary support for their future development.

Pigs will have to face a strong challenger in their love affairs this month. However, they should be patient in dealing with this matter. It would be much better for them to wait for a while, because they will be very sorry for any hasty decisions at this stage.

Pigs will have nothing to worry about regarding their health this month, but they must try to keep away from cliffs and high walls. They have to keep in mind that it is better to be safe than sorry.

The Ninth Month (8 October – 6 November)

Miracles sometimes occur, but one has to work terribly hard for them

It will be quite difficult for Pigs to make major breakthroughs at work this month because of the appearance of several Unlucky Stars within their Sign. However, they might be able to create a miracle if they really try their best to work for that. Determination will play a vital part in their success at work this month. In addition, good personal and business relationships will increase their chances of success.

Pigs will be quite passionate this month. There will be endless troubles in the months to come if Pigs can't control their emotions and passions properly. They must try to turn down sex temptations firmly at month's end, or their careers will be spoiled.

This will be one of the most fortunate months in money affairs for the Pig. If Pigs want to buy property or luxuries for themselves, this month is the most suitable time to do so. If they are looking for investment opportunities, they should try to take the action now.

The Tenth Month (7 November – 6 December)

A light heart lives long

Pigs will be able to overcome almost all difficulties in front of them this month. They have reason to be optimistic, and they should apply their optimistic attitude at work and in dealing with the people around them throughout the month. Their optimism will make dull reality light up with sparkles. It would be a big help for their success if Pigs can cheer up fellow-workers. Since Pigs will be quite persuasive this month, it will be possible for them to reach a very important agreement with clients this month.

The relationship between Pigs and their lovers will be much improved this month. They will be able to enjoy a very sweet and romantic month. Actually, this month is a good time for Pigs to take a vacation. They will travel quite frequently this month.

Pigs will be able to get satisfactory returns from their investments this month. Occasionally they will have some luck in lottery and gambling, but they should not get too greedy. The fortune of Pigs will drop down sharply in the next two months, so they must try to save more money for the coming rainy days.

The Eleventh Month (7 December – 4 January)

There's no great loss without some gain

Pigs will suffer a great deal from numerous disputes and problems at work this month. Unless they are willing to put more time and effort in to improve the situation, Pigs will end up with nothing at year end. Most important of all, Pigs should try not to be blinded by ambition or arrogance. Pigs will have a better chance of success if they wish to start a new business in a foreign land, especially if they look to the East or Northeast.

Pigs seems to be quite fortunate at the beginning of the month. However, if they become too ambitious and greedy, they will meet with a very sad ending. Just as the old saying goes, 'There's no great loss without some gain.' Pigs should try not to be too ambitious or greedy this month.

Pigs will be bothered very much by rumours and gossip about their love affairs. No matter what happens, Pigs should never cheat on their lovers this month. If they play with fire, they will surely get burned.

The Twelfth Month (5 January – 3 February)

A penny saved is a penny earned

Although the fortune of Pigs will improve somewhat this month, they still have to work very hard to survive in their careers. They should not be reluctant to make some renovations if there are major weaknesses found. Their original business systems and procedures are probably somewhat outdated. Pigs must have the guts to make revolutionary changes. It would be much better for them to do so before it gets too late. Apart from this, Pigs have to watch their budget when making their business plan, to avoid over-expansion.

There will be several unexpected expenses for Pigs this month. Unless they have saved enough beforehand, Pigs will be in deep trouble.

Pigs should keep in mind that thrift is a great revenue; the more money saved, the more money earned.

The health of Pigs is improving this month, but it would be much better if they can cut out their bad habits such as heavy smoking and drinking. Their first taste of drugs will lead them nowhere but down the road to total destruction.

Using Feng Shui to Improve Fortune: Directions, Colours, Numbers and Lucky Charm

The ancient Chinese used the traditional Horoscope to predict their fortune on a yearly basis – they used the art of Feng Shui to improve their luck.

It was their belief that the application of tactical Feng Shui would change their bad luck into good, and make their good luck improve even more.

This same method is still effective in today's modern world.

There are four main elements which I will use in tactical Feng Shui:

◆ Lucky Directions
◆ Lucky Colours
◆ Lucky Numbers
◆ Lucky Charm

This will not be a very good year for Pigs, both in career and money matters. They should try to be more conservative in handling these matters. In addition they should try to change their old attitudes and procedures in business if they want to survive. Probably they would have better luck in foreign places. They should never try to get into any illegal business, or they will surely end up behind bars. Pigs can hardly expect to have too much luck in gambling and investments. Pigs will not be so healthy this year, and they must cut out their bad habits such as heavy smoking and drinking. This is definitely not a romantic year for the Pig.

I would suggest applying the following Feng Shui tactics to improve luck so that Pigs don't have to worry too much about their fate within the year.

Lucky Directions

The most favourable directions of the year for the Pig are **South**, **Southwest** and **Northeast**. Pigs should sleep or sit in these directions if they wish to improve their fortune.

To make this procedure very simple, divide the house or room into nine imaginary squares. Then, using a compass, check the exact direction of each square as shown in Figure 7. This will help to ensure that you do not make a mistake with the direction.

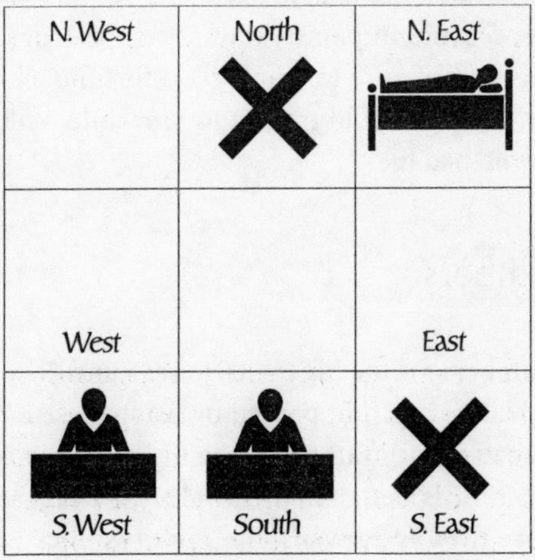

Figure 7

Pigs should sit in the relevant directions at work or while studying; this will ensure that their achievements are much greater than the Stars intended. To improve health and achieve a good night's sleep, Pigs should position their bed in the favourable direction shown (Northeast).

However, the Pig should try to keep away from the un-favourable directions of the year; that is, Southeast and North as shown in Figure 7. The Pig should try not to sit, work or sleep in these directions, in order to get rid of the negative influences lurking there.

Lucky Colours

According to Chinese tradition, each of the five elements has its own representative colours. Fire is represented by red, pink and purple, Earth by yellow and brown, and so on. As a Feng Shui Master I would suggest **green**, **red**, **pink** and **purple** as the Pig's lucky colours for the year 2001.

Use these colours in paints, wall coverings, rugs, drapes and curtains. This will be sure to bring good fortune within the year.

However, the Pig should try not to use white, yellow or brown in 2001, to avoid bad luck.

Lucky Numbers

The lucky numbers for the Pig in 2001 are: **5** and **7**.

Fortune will be much improved by using these lucky numbers whenever possible. For example, if the Pig has a choice, the phone number 257-5277 is better than 256-4272 – because the former contains more fives and sevens, the Pig's two lucky numbers for the year.

Lucky Charm

Feng Shui Masters believe that special objects can be used as a medium between human beings and nature. The fortune of the recipient is greatly improved as the positive wave of energy from nature is passed through the object or 'lucky charm' on to the recipient.

The lucky charm for the Pig in 2001 is a green and red stone carving with four turtles going for a stream of clear water from four corners, as shown below. For the best result, this stone carving should be placed in the south or the southwest direction of the house.

Chapter Eight

The
Mouse

Years of the Mouse

1912 (5/Feb/12—3/Feb/13)   1960 (5/Feb/60—3/Feb/61)
1924 (5/Feb/24—3/Feb/25)   1972 (5/Feb/72—3/Feb/73)
1936 (5/Feb/36—3/Feb/37)   1984 (4/Feb/84—3/Feb/84)
1948 (5/Feb/48—3/Feb/49)   1996 (4/Feb/96—3/Feb/97)

Distribution of the Stars within the Sign for 2001

Lucky Stars	Unlucky Stars
Jade Hall	Sudden Collapse
Dragon's Virtue	Heavenly Hazards
Crape Myrtle	Six Harms

Lucky Stars
Jade Hall

In ancient China, thousands and thousands of scholars prepared
for the Civil Service Examinations. However, only a few hundred

of them ever passed and would consequently be admitted to the ruling class. This newly-promoted elite would be deeply honoured with a big feast in a large decorated jade hall to celebrate their brilliant success.

When this Star appears, people will do well in their studies and in their work. They will have an important breakthrough if they work at it.

Dragon's Virtue

Virtue was highly appreciated by Confucius. The ancient Chinese believed that virtue not only set a good example to others, but provided its own good results. Of the four 'Virtue' Stars in the Chinese Horoscope, 'Dragon's Virtue' is one of the most important.

Since for centuries the dragon was regarded as a symbol of the Emperor, the 'Dragon's Virtue' signified the Emperor's virtue and goodness, which would benefit the entire empire and its people.

When this Star appears, people will have a successful and productive year. They will get support from other people, especially their subordinates.

Crape Myrtle

Since the flower Crape Myrtle was deliberately planted inside the royal courts of the Forbidden City, it became known as the Emperor's flower. Later, it came to symbolize superiority within the feudal hierarchy.

People under this Star will easily get major promotions, and will have the authority and confidence to overcome all difficulties and opposition they may face.

Unlucky Stars

Sudden Collapse

A building, project or business will ultimately collapse if it lacks a solid foundation – one which must be steadily maintained. 'Sudden Collapse', as its name suggests, is considered to be a bad omen. In order to prevent this kind of tragedy, people have to build up their foundation slowly but surely.

When this Star appears within a Sign, people have to watch out for the economic growth of their business, and for sudden changes such as a dramatic drop in sales and production or cancellation of contracts, etc.

Heavenly Hazards

The ancient Chinese believed that the gods in heaven would deliberately confront people with difficult obstacles in life to test them. Those who failed to pass these dangerous tests, it was believed, would be given a miserable life. Not surprisingly, this Star is considered to be a bad omen.

When this Star appears, people will face many challenges, which they must overcome if they want to avoid losing out.

Six Harms

To the ancient Chinese peasants, floods, drought, frost, wars, plagues of locusts and other insects and so on were the major harms faced by their crops. The occurrence of any one of these harms would seriously damage their income. The appearance of the Star 'Six Harms' is a very bad omen to the economy of the people concerned.

When this Star appears within a Sign, people have to watch out for the economic growth of their business, and for sudden changes such as a dramatic drop in sales and production or cancellation of contracts, etc.

General Overview of the Year

Generally speaking, this will be a very productive year for the Mouse. Mice will be quite successful in different kinds of examinations and interviews. Their diligence and intelligence will impress their superiors, and therefore be promoted. However, Mice should try to keep a low profile in order to eliminate unnecessary trouble from jealous people around them.

Financially this won't be a profitable year for Mice, and they have to watch their budget and economic growth very carefully.

Mice should not expect too much from romance, or they will be deeply disappointed.

Fortunately, Mice will be quite healthy this year, and have nothing to worry about on this score.

Career   ＊＊＊＊
Money   ＊＊
Health   ＊＊＊
Love   ＊

＊＊＊＊ = Very Fortunate/＊＊＊ = Pretty Good/＊＊ = Fair/＊ = Unsatisfactory

Career ＊＊＊＊

Mice will be quite productive this year, but they should try to keep a low profile if they want to face fewer obstacles on their way to success. Their humble attitude will not only win the whole-hearted support of their subordinates, but will also help them to be free from the frequent attacks and abuse from jealous people around them. Fortunately, Mice will have enough confidence and ability to overcome numerous challenges at work.

Mice will be able to do much better in their business during the third, seventh, eighth and the last three months of the year, so they should try to make good use of these months if they want to have a successful year.

Money ＊＊

The Mouse won't have too much luck in money affairs this year. Although their business is running smoothly throughout the year, Mice must pay special attention to their business' economic growth or they will suffer a lot of money problems. Mice may experience a sudden collapse in business due to over-expansion or over-expenditure. Mice will have better luck during the second and tenth month. But they must keep alert to money affairs during the first, fourth, sixth, ninth and the last month of the year.

Health ***

The health of the Mouse will be in a satisfactory condition this year. However, Mice have to watch their diets during the first, second, sixth, eighth and the last month of the year. Apart from this, Mice should watch their home safety very carefully this year. They should pay special attention to fire hazards at home, especially in the fourth and fifth month. It would be much better for them not to stay out very late at night on the streets, to avoid being hurt or robbed. Most important of all, Mice must try their best to resist the temptation of drugs this year, especially during the eleventh month.

Love *

Unfortunately, this won't be a romantic year for the Mouse. Consequently they should not expect too much on this front, or they will be deeply disappointed. Mice should take it easy in love affairs, or their aggressiveness will just scare their lovers away. However, Mice will have relatively better luck in romance on the first, seventh, tenth and the last month of the year. They may, however, face a broken relationship during the fourth, fifth and the eleventh month, so Mice should try to calm themselves down and not have serious quarrels with their lovers during these three months.

According to traditional Chinese astrology, the distributions of the Lucky and Unlucky Stars within a Sign will more or less determine a person's fate in a particular year. Just as the distributions of the Stars change from year to year, however, they also change from month to month. Each Sign's fate for the year and for each month is calculated according to this basic rule.

Monthly In-depth Forecasts
The First Month (4 February – 4 March)

Business before pleasure

The Mouse will be very active in different kinds of social activities, and this will occupy a lot of their time. Mice should try to manage their schedules properly if they wish to be more successful in their studies and careers. This month will be a very romantic period of time for Mice, and they will enjoy this very much. However, they should try to restrain themselves and not let things get out of control, or they will face endless troubles.

Mice should watch their diets carefully this month, and try to keep away from the temptations of delicious food and good wine.

This is not a good time for Mice to try their luck at gambling. By month's end Mice will realize they've spent more money than they'd thought, and this will lead them into an embarrassing situation. Apart from this, Mice should watch out for pick-pockets, especially at the beginning of the month.

The Second Month (5 March – 4 April)

The sea never refuses water

Mice should try to make good use of available time for further studies in order to equip themselves with better knowledge in different areas. The knowledge they are picking up now may seem meaningless, but it might become very helpful to their careers in the near future. Apart from this, Mice should not bind themselves to their usual duties and planning, because this month is a very good time for them to make some necessary changes.

In social gatherings Mice should not turn a cold shoulder to any new acquaintance, or they will be very sorry very soon. Just keep in mind the old saying, 'It takes all sorts to make a world.' In other words, Mice should be more open to different kinds of friends, ideas and work within this period of time. This will help them to have a more successful and productive year.

Mice should watch their diets, and especially keep away from raw foods near the end of the month. No matter how busy they are, Mice should not ignore their lovers. A bunch of flowers, an impressive love letter or a romantic dinner will bring a very nice surprise their way.

The Third Month (5 April – 4 May)

A bird never flew on one wing

Mice will be very successful and productive in the first three months of the year if they try their best in their careers. However, they have to find good partners or they will spoil the whole thing. Without a capable partner with good faith, Mice will be as helpless as an eagle flying with just one wing. The main concern this month is to try to improve personal and business relations, in order to win the necessary support whenever needed. Mice should watch out for attacks from hidden enemies. These attacks won't damage them if they keep a careful eye out.

Fortunately, the luck of the Mouse in money affairs will be much improved this month. Mice will have an abundant income from different sources, and their investments will see satisfactory returns within this period of time.

Mice will feel lonely at heart even though there are plenty of people around them. They should try to relax and enjoy life without too much complaining, or they will end up isolated sooner or later.

The Fourth Month (5 May – 4 June)

There's no smoke without fire

The fortune of Mice will drop sharply this month, so they should keep alert to sudden drops in business or economic growth. A strong opponent may try to challenge them, so they have to prepare themselves properly. Mice may hear some warnings about their job and money affairs – they shouldn't overlook these or they will receive a severe shock.

There will be rumours flying around about their romance; Mice should not hide their head in the sand. As the old saying goes, 'There's no smoke without fire.' Mice should try to locate the source of the smoke and put the fire out before it is too late.

Basically, health is satisfactory this month. However, Mice should mind their personal safety – specifically, they must try not to stay out too late at night to avoid being hurt or robbed.

The Fifth Month (5 June – 6 July)

If you play with fire, you get burned

Mice have to pay special attention to their home safety, especially regarding fire. They should of course never let their children play with fire.

Mice should handle their work properly and legally, because any illegal action will only bring sad consequences for their business. They should stop indulging in dirty tricks, and try to follow the rules of the game closely if they don't want to get burned.

This is definitely not a suitable time for Mice to start new business or investment projects. They will face a lot of trouble and difficulties right from the beginning if they insist on doing so. They'd better wait a few months, when they'll have more luck in these matters.

Mice should try to keep calm about their romance. They should never start a quarrel with their lovers, or they will be very sorry very soon. They should walk away for a while until they can control themselves emotionally.

The Sixth Month (7 July – 6 August)

Be patient and endure

The Mice's fortune is changing for the better this month. However, they should proceed step by step in business, in order to avoid a sudden big fall. Again, Mice should not play dirty tricks or they will hurt no one but themselves. Somebody may try to provoke them and then try to take advantage of this, so Mice should try to keep calm and not lose their wisdom in the heat of their anger. If they want to keep their business on the right track, Mice should try to be patient and wait for the right moment to take the correct action.

There will be some money traps in front of them, so Mice should keep their eyes wide open to avoid them. Mice should never let their greediness blind them when investing or gambling, or they will lose a lot of money.

Health will be not so good this month. It would be wise if Mice went to see a doctor for a check-up if there is anything amiss. Their health will be much improved if they follow doctor's orders carefully.

The Seventh Month (7 August – 6 September)

There is always room at the top

Mice will enjoy much better luck in the latter part of the year, so they should try to put more effort and time into upgrading their business now. They will be very successful and productive by doing so. Their efforts will be deeply appreciated by their superiors, and they will be promoted as a result. Mice should not worry about their future prospects, because there is always room at the top.

However, they should keep a low profile in order to avoid unnecessary trouble, or they will surely be bothered very much by the jealous people around them. Mice are able to achieve high scores in their examinations this month if they really work hard enough.

Health is much better this month, but Mice to watch their personal safety when they go out to the countryside.

Mice should keep their eyes wide open this month if they are looking for a new romance. They should try to grasp this rare opportunity without any hesitation, because it will slip away as quickly as lightning.

The Eighth Month (7 September – 7 October)

Silence is golden

The Mouse will have a very good imagination this month. Mice will be quite creative if they can organize all their ideas in a practical and positive manner. In addition, they should ask professional advice from experts if they want to be more successful. Many opportunities will knock at the door within this period of time, and Mice should try their best to choose the most suitable one and forget all about the others. Concentration is the key to their success. However, Mice should not talk too much about work to avoid leaking any secrets, or their opponents will take advantage of this and have the chance to beat them.

Mice should try to cut their talkative habit in social gatherings, since rumour and gossip will only bring them serious trouble in the near future. Just like the old saying goes, 'Words are a loaded pistol.'

Mice will suffer from digestive problems this month, such as stomach ache and possibly food poisoning. Therefore, they should watch the cleanliness of their food and must keep away from raw or unhygienic foods.

The Ninth Month (8 October – 6 November)

Bad news travels fast

Rumours and gossip will keep on bothering Mice this month. Mice should try to quash these as soon as possible, because bad news travels fast. They must have the courage to stand up firmly to clarify their position whenever needed. Honesty is the best policy in handling business this month, because this will eliminate a lot of misunderstanding and trouble. It is very important for Mice to get the whole-hearted support of subordinates, or they will become the helpless victims of their opponents.

Health is changing for the better this month. The only concern has to do with the health of younger family members. Mice should try to find a doctor to take care of their children at once in case anything goes amiss. Any delays will be quite dangerous.

Fortunes fluctuate this month, so Mice should not try their luck at gambling, nor would this be a good time to buy any property.

The Tenth Month (7 November – 6 December)

Laugh and the world laughs with you

Almost all the Mouse's troubles will be gone with the wind this month. Mice can concentrate on their careers again without too many distractions. The last three months of the year will be a very good time for Mice to start new projects or business pursuits, because they will be more creative and productive within this period. Humour and laughter rather than seriousness and stiffness will bring nice surprises this month, so Mice should maintain a pleasant manner at work.

Fortune is changing for the better this month. Mice will be able to realize good profits from their investments within this period. Occasionally Mice will have luck in lottery and gambling, but they should not get too greedy.

There will be an important breakthrough in romance for Mice at the end of the month. If they can be nice and considerate towards their lovers, Mice will enjoy a very sweet and romantic response in return.

The Eleventh Month (7 December – 4 January)

You don't get something for nothing

There will be some obstacles on the way to success, so Mice should keep alert to any warnings and try to take the necessary precautionary measures as soon as possible. Mice should never try to rely on others to overcome their difficulties for them. Instead, they should try to stand up firmly for themselves. Mice will see hardly any achievements this month unless they are willing to put in the extra time and effort. They should keep in mind that you don't get something for nothing.

The Mouse will be quite healthy physically and mentally this month. But Mice should firmly reject the temptation of drugs. If possible, they should try not to stay out late on the streets to avoid being hurt or robbed.

Mice should not expect too much in romance this month, or they will be deeply disappointed. Their aggressiveness will just scare their lovers away.

The Twelfth Month (5 January – 3 February)

Stretch no further than your arms will reach

Mice will be quite busy and productive this month, but they should not be too ambitious. Over-confidence will blind their eyes and make them lose their focus. Mice should keep in mind that they should never make any expansions beyond their ability and budget, or they will tumble down from their positions this month.

Mice must pay special attention to the economic growth of their business this month. If not, they may face a sudden collapse in their business due to over-expansion or over-expenditure.

The Mouse's romantic life will turn to a new page this month. Mice should show their affection properly from time to time in order to maintain this delicate relationship. It would be much better if Mice can keep a low profile in their love affairs and keep any romance a secret at this stage.

Using Feng Shui to Improve Fortune: Directions, Colours, Numbers and Lucky Charm

The ancient Chinese used the traditional Horoscope to predict their fortune on a yearly basis – they used the art of Feng Shui to improve their luck.

It was their belief that the application of tactical Feng Shui would change their bad luck into good, and make their good luck improve even more.

This same method is still effective in today's modern world.

There are four main elements which I will use in tactical Feng Shui:

◆ Lucky Directions
◆ Lucky Colours
◆ Lucky Numbers
◆ Lucky Charm

This will be a very productive year for the Mouse. Mice will see important breakthroughs in their careers if they work hard enough. They will be promoted due to their diligence and intelligence. However, they should try to avoid over-expanding and over-expenditure. Mice will be quite healthy this year, but they should not expect too much in love affairs.

I would suggest applying the following Feng Shui tactics to improve luck so that Mice don't have to worry too much about their fate within the year.

Lucky Directions

The most favourable directions of the year for the Mouse are **Southeast**, **Southwest** and **Northeast**. Mice should sleep or sit in these directions if they wish to improve their fortune.

To make this procedure very simple, divide the house or room into nine imaginary squares. Then, using a compass, check the exact direction of each square as shown in Figure 8. This will help to ensure that you do not make a mistake with the direction.

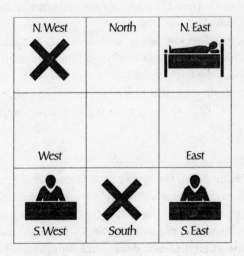

Figure 8

Mice should sit in the relevant directions at work or while study-ing; this will ensure that their achievements are much greater than the Stars intended. To improve health and achieve a good night's sleep, Mice should position their bed in the favourable direction shown (Northeast).

However, the Mouse should try to keep away from the unfavourable directions of the year; that is, South and Northwest as shown in Figure 8. The Mouse should try not to sit, work or sleep in these directions, in order to get rid of the negative influences lurking there.

Lucky Colours

According to Chinese tradition, each of the five elements has its own representative colours. Fire is represented by red, pink and purple, Earth by yellow and brown, and so on. As a Feng Shui Master I would suggest **blue**, **grey**, **black** and **green** as the Mouse's lucky colours for the year 2001.

Use these colours in paints, wall coverings, rugs, drapes and curtains. This will be sure to bring good fortune within the year.

However, the Mouse should try not to use white, red, pink or purple in 2001, to avoid bad luck.

Lucky Numbers

The lucky numbers for the Mouse in 2001 are: **5** and **9**.

Fortune will be much improved by using these lucky numbers whenever possible. For example, if the Mouse has a choice, the phone number 595-3599 is better than 647-4711 – because the former contains more fives and nines, the Mouse's two lucky numbers for the year.

Lucky Charm

Feng Shui Masters believe that special objects can be used as a medium between human beings and nature. The fortune of the recipient is greatly improved as the positive wave of energy from nature is passed through the object or 'lucky charm' on to the recipient.

The lucky charm for the Mouse in 2001 is a green circular carving with three carps embracing a big pearl together with their bodies, as shown below. For the best result, this green carving should be placed in the southeast or the southwest direction of the house.

Chapter Nine

The

Ox

Years of the Ox

1913 (4/Feb/13—3/Feb/14)   1961 (4/Feb/61—3/Feb/62)
1925 (4/Feb/25—3/Feb/26)   1973 (4/Feb/73—3/Feb/74)
1937 (4/Feb/37—3/Feb/38)   1985 (4/Feb/85—3/Feb/86)
1949 (4/Feb/49—3/Feb/50)   1997 (4/Feb/97—3/Feb/98)

Distribution of the Stars within the Sign for 2001

Lucky Stars   Unlucky Stars

None   Fierce Hercules
       Heavenly Weeping
       White Tiger
       Yellow Funeral Flag
       Decorative Top

Unlucky Stars

Fierce Hercules

Fei Lian is the name of a famous Chinese Hercules who served the wicked Emperor Zhou of the Shang Dynasty. His hot temper and tremendous energy brought considerable destruction to his people. To live in peace they tried to keep out of his way and not irritate him.

The appearance of this Star is a bad omen. People will be seriously hurt physically and financially if they provoke their superiors.

Heavenly Weeping

The ancient Chinese believed that Heaven was capable of reacting to and being sensitive towards the experiences and plight of those on earth. If the people suffered from starvation and violence, then Heaven would weep for them. Thus, the appearance of 'Heavenly Weeping' indicates troubles.

When this Star appears, people will face a lot of problems and will have to struggle hard to get out from under them.

White Tiger

In ancient China, it was the tiger, and not the lion, who was considered king of the jungle. The white tiger was the most fierce and feared of all tigers, and gradually became a symbol of violence and danger.

When this Star appears, people need to stay alert for danger and sudden attacks, which could turn them into helpless victims.

Yellow Funeral Flag

In ancient times, the Chinese believed that the spirits of the newly dead floated aimlessly in the sky. To guide the spirits back home, their families would fly a yellow flag from the rooftop to signal where they lived. Not surprisingly, yellow flags soon become the symbol for death and funerals.

When this Star appears, people need to be extra careful about the health and safety of younger family members. Keep in mind that 'prevention is better than cure.'

Decorative Top

In ancient China, only the nobles and important people were allowed to cover the tops of their carriages with rich decoration, which varied according to rank. Such decorated carriages naturally became associated with high social status, luxury and, interestingly enough, with a certain degree of isolation typical of those who inhabit their own exclusive world away from the masses.

Thus, the implications of this Star are ambiguous. On one hand, when this Star appears people will enjoy a successful year; on the other, they will have a tendency to become isolated if they do not remain connected in their personal relationships.

General Overview of the Year

This won't be a smooth year for Oxen, and they will face numerous challenges and difficulties at work. Therefore, they should be more conservative in handling their business or they will end up very sorry by year's end. Most important of all, Oxen should never try their luck in anything illegal, as they will surely be punished. Although they will have a steady income, they should not risk their money in gambling. Their main concern is not how to earn money, but how to save money.

Oxen will have not too much to worry about regarding their health this year, but they must mind the health and safety of their children.

Oxen should try to build a better understanding with their lovers this year, before it's too late.

Career   *
Money   ***
Health   **
Love   **

*** = Pretty Good/** = Fair/* = Unsatisfactory

Career *

Oxen must try to be more cautious and conservative in handling their business. It would be much better if Oxen wish to content themselves with their own reasonable shares only, because their ambitions and aggressiveness within the year will only lead them to destruction. To make the situation even worse, Oxen will be somewhat isolated by their colleagues if they refuse to change their self-centred attitude. Most important of all, Oxen must not get involved in any illegal activities this year, or they will surely be punished. The most practical solution is to turn down all these kinds of temptations firmly, without hesitation. Oxen will face a lot of troubles and difficulties during the first, second, sixth, seventh, tenth and the last month of the year. Oxen must really try to put more time and effort in at work during these months if they want to survive in their chosen career. On the other hand, Oxen will have better opportunities at work during the fourth, fifth, eighth and eleventh month. Oxen will be in a better position in their careers if they can make good use of these four months.

Money ***

Although Oxen won't have too much luck in money affairs this year, they won't have to worry too much because they will enjoy a steady income in spite of the fact that their business will not be so prosperous. The most fortunate months for Oxen are the third, fourth, seventh, eighth and the eleventh. However, they should take good care of their money during the first, second, sixth and the tenth month of the year. Generally speaking, their main concern this year is not how to earn more money, but how to save more money.

Health **

Fortunately, the health of Oxen will be not bad at all, and they needn't worry too much about it. However, they have to watch their road safety during the fifth month, and try to keep away from dangerous places during the seventh month. Oxen have to take good care of their children at home during the second, ninth and tenth month. They should keep in mind that their children must have proper medical treatment as soon as accidents or injuries happen.

Love **

Romance seems quite good for Oxen in the first part of the year, but things will take a down-turn towards year end. Oxen should try to build up a better mutual understanding with their lovers before it's too late. Oxen will have better luck in love affairs during the first, fourth and the eleventh month. On the other hand, romance will be threatened on the second, sixth, seventh, ninth, tenth and the last month of the year. Oxen may face a broken relationship with their lovers if they can't handle their love affairs properly during these six months.

According to traditional Chinese astrology, the distributions of the Lucky and Unlucky Stars within a Sign will more or less determine a person's fate in a particular year. Just as the distributions of the Stars change from year to year, however, they also change from month to month. Each Sign's fate for the year and for each month is calculated according to this basic rule.

Monthly In-depth Forecasts
The First Month (4 February – 4 March)

A little knowledge is a dangerous thing

Oxen will face different kinds of problems in their career this month, and they'd be best off seeking advice and assistance from experts or experienced seniors, because the problems they are going to face will be most likely beyond their control. They will probably just mess things up if Oxen try to solve these problems all by themselves. Just like the old saying goes, 'A little knowledge is a dangerous thing.' Oxen should admit their inexperience in certain areas because any pretence will bring nothing but a destructive outcome.

This won't be a fortunate month for Oxen in money affairs. They will be big losers if they try their luck in gambling or any high-risk investments. They should try to control their budget.

Fortunately, Oxen will have a wonderful time with their lovers this month. However, Oxen should not indulge themselves too much in love because there will be a lot of other things for them to manage. If they do not find a balance, both career and romance will be spoiled in the near future.

The Second Month (5 March – 4 April)

He who rides a tiger is afraid to dismount

Different kinds of problems are still chasing Oxen this month. Patience and caution will be the two important tools to help them get out of trouble. One thing Oxen should bear in mind is that they should never give up, as they won't get a second chance to put things right. They have to fight to the finish and never say die. There may be some career breakthroughs in the latter part of the year if they have really tried their best at work.

There will be some misunderstandings between Oxen and their lovers. They should never overlook this situation or they will end up very sorry very soon. This is definitely not a romantic month for Oxen.

Oxen should take good care of the younger members of their family. They should never leave children alone at home, and must keep all knives and scissors in a safe place out of the way.

The Third Month (5 April – 4 May)

Do right and fear no man

The fortune of Oxen will change for the better from the beginning of the month. Now's the time for them to think about their future development. The better they plan for themselves, the better they will be later in the year. Oxen should not be too humble when facing strong opponents. All they have to do is get on with their own job properly, then they will be unbeatable. Someone may try to scare them away, but Oxen should not give up under any circumstances.

Their investments may bring satisfactory returns to them at the end of the month, yet Oxen should not be too ambitious in money matters. They have to watch for money traps very carefully.

Oxen will be quite popular, but unfortunately they will be deeply disappointed if they are looking for true love this month.

The Fourth Month (5 May – 4 June)

Good things come in small packages

This is one of the most favourable months of the year for Oxen. They must try to make good use of this period of time if they wish to see some achievements at work, or they will be left empty-handed at year end. Better personal relationships will give Oxen a big boost in their success at work. If they want to make any changes in their jobs Oxen should do it now, or they will miss a very good opportunity.

This will be a profitable month for Oxen. They will have luck in lottery and gambling. Apart from this, they will receive income from a new source.

Oxen will be in a very good shape physically and mentally, but they have to watch their road safety. They should walk and drive with extreme care during the last five days of the month.

The Fifth Month (5 June – 6 July)

Too many cooks spoil the broth

This month is a very suitable time for Oxen to carry out new projects, but they should try to be more independent in making decisions. This means they should try to make their own decisions even though some other people may try to interfere. Just as the old saying goes, 'Too many cooks spoil the broth.' Oxen should turn down any interference politely if they don't want to mess up their work. Apart from this, this is not a good period of time to accept new partners, or there will be endless personal disputes in the months to come.

Oxen should watch out for the appearance of a third person between their lovers and them. Things will become more and more complicated, so they should try to settle any problems calmly at this very early stage.

Oxen will be able to make profits this month if they are taking care of their money by themselves. The story will be quite different, however, if they are making money with some other people.

The Sixth Month (7 July – 6 August)

Of two evils, choose the lesser

Again, difficulties and disputes will chase after Oxen like shadows this month, as they did in the first two months of the year. Oxen should keep alert to any possible solutions, or their careers will be in jeopardy. This month, Oxen will find that they are caught up in a dilemma and won't know which way to go, and the situation will become worse and worse as time goes by. Oxen should try their best to make decisions as quickly as possible. When they are trying to make up their mind, Oxen should keep this old saying in mind as a guide: 'Of two evils, choose the lesser.'

Relations between Oxen and their lovers will become more and more complicated this month. Unless they can build up a better mutual understanding, the whole thing will end very sadly very soon.

This month is definitely not a good time for Oxen to risk their money in any kind of gambling or investment. They should watch their expenses closely to make sure they don't run out of money.

The Seventh Month (7 August – 6 September)

God helps those who help themselves

Although the fortune of Oxen sees some improvement this month, they will face severe career tests right now. They can rely on nobody but themselves in this situation. They have to stand up firmly and never give up under any circumstances. They have to keep in mind that 'God helps those who help themselves.' It would be much better if Oxen can reach a compromise with superiors or opponents.

The economic situation will improve this month. However, it is still necessary for Oxen to keep a tight rein on their budget. They should not lend money, because they will never see it again.

This will not be a good time for Oxen to go out on any kind of adventures. Personal safety is their main concern this month, so they should try to keep away from dangerous places.

The Eighth Month (7 September – 7 October)

It takes all kinds to make a world

This is one of the most favourable months of the year for Oxen, so they should try to make good use of this chance to improve their work. Their efforts during this period will be handsomely rewarded. Most important of all, Oxen should be more open and generous if they want to be more successful. This means they should try to accept different kinds of talents and ideas regarding their projects, as these will prove to be tremendous contributions to their success. Otherwise they will be badly defeated as a result of isolation and their own inflated self-opinion.

There will be some friends coming for a visit from foreign places unexpectedly near month's end. Oxen should never talk about politics or religion with these friends, to avoid unnecessary quarrels. Nor should they drink too much with their old friends, or they will be very sorry in the months to come.

This is a profitable month for Oxen. They will have some luck in lottery and gambling. But they should take care of their wallets, and watch out for pick-pockets.

The Ninth Month (8 October – 6 November)

Faith moves mountains

There will be some important changes at work this month. The sooner Oxen acquaint themselves with these new changes, the more successful they will be in the near future. Otherwise, they will become helpless victims of these new circumstances. Oxen should keep in mind that 'Honesty is the best policy.' They can impress and persuade even the most stubborn opponents by being honest during this period. On the other hand, any cheating or unscrupulous behaviour will only bring terrible consequences.

Oxen should never lie to their lovers, because cheats never prosper, especially this month. On the other hand, their faith in love will deeply impress their lovers and bring them a nice surprise eventually.

Oxen should take good care of their children at home. They must try to keep them away from sharp objects, fire and hot water.

The Tenth Month (7 November – 6 December)

Better safe than sorry

This is one of the months that Oxen should keep alert to possible danger. Their main concern this month is the safety of their children and themselves. Oxen should not stay out late on the streets to avoid possible robbery and street violence. Apart from this, they should watch their road safety carefully, especially in the middle of the month, or they will end up very sorry indeed. Oxen should never neglect the safety of their children at home this month. They must keep their children well away from hot water, fire and any sharp objects. Better safe than sorry.

Finances fluctuate within this period, so it would not be wise for Oxen to try their luck with gambling or high-risk investments. They must turn down all temptations of this kind firmly and absolutely.

This will not be a good time for Oxen to make any dramatic changes in their career. They should try to keep a low profile for self-preservation.

The Eleventh Month (7 December – 4 January)

Will wonders never cease

Although Oxen will face numerous obstacles at work, they might have a chance of some real breakthroughs if they try hard enough. Success or failure within this month will depend mainly on their own determination and effort. They will be the master of their fate within this period of time. However, Oxen should never try to challenge their superiors or strong enemies this month, to avoid unnecessary trouble.

The luck of Oxen will be much improved this month. They will have a steady income from different sources. Their main concern is not how to earn money, but how to save money.

Oxen will meet their dream-lovers this month. Unless they are courageous enough to express their affections properly, they will miss out on a very good chance. Oxen should summon up their courage, because there's nothing to lose even if they end up rejected.

The Twelfth Month (5 January – 3 February)

What goes up must come down

This month will not be a good time for Oxen to carry out new projects, as they will meet with a lot of opposition and difficulty. It's better for them to stay in their own position and get on with their own business. Their ambition and aggressiveness this month will lead them only to destruction. If Oxen are eagerly trying to climb to a higher position by means of dirty tricks, they are sure to have a big fall in the near future.

Oxen should not be too greedy in any kind of investment this month, or they will suffer a big loss. They should try to keep a tight budget to avoid over-expenditure, both in business and family economics.

Health will become unstable within this period, so they should go and see a doctor for medical treatment at the first sign of trouble.

Using Feng Shui to Improve Fortune: Directions, Colours, Numbers and Lucky Charm

The ancient Chinese used the traditional Horoscope to predict their fortune on a yearly basis – they used the art of Feng Shui to improve their luck.

It was their belief that the application of tactical Feng Shui would change their bad luck into good, and make their good luck improve even more.

This same method is still effective in today's modern world.

There are four main elements which I will use in tactical Feng Shui:

◆ Lucky Directions
◆ Lucky Colours
◆ Lucky Numbers
◆ Lucky Charm

This won't be a smooth year for Oxen, because they will face numerous challenges and difficulties. They should be more conservative in handling their business, or there will be a sudden collapse. Most important of all, Oxen should never try their luck in any illegal affairs since they will be surely punished for that. Financially, the main concern for Oxen is not how to earn, but how to save money. Fortunately, their health will be not too bad. Oxen should try their best to build up a better understanding with their lovers before it's too late.

I would suggest applying the following Feng Shui tactics to improve luck so that Oxen don't have to worry too much about their fate within the year.

Lucky Directions

The most favourable directions of the year for Oxen are **Southeast**, **West** and **North**. Oxen should sleep or sit in these directions if they wish to improve their fortune.

To make this procedure very simple, divide the house or room into nine imaginary squares. Then, using a compass, check the exact direction of each square as shown in Figure 9. This will help to ensure that you do not make a mistake with the direction.

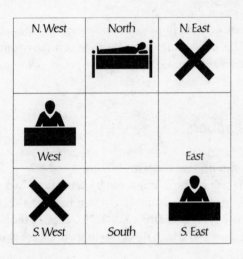

Figure 9

Oxen should sit in the relevant directions at work or while studying; this will ensure that achievements are much greater than the Stars intended. To improve health and achieve a good night's sleep, Oxen should position their bed in the favourable direction shown (North).

However, Oxen should try to keep away from the unfavourable directions of the year; that is, Southwest and Northeast as shown in Figure 9. Oxen should try not to sit, work or sleep in these directions, in order to get rid of the negative influences lurking there.

Lucky Colours

According to Chinese tradition, each of the five elements has its own representative colours. Fire is represented by red, pink and purple, Earth by yellow and brown, and so on. As a Feng Shui Master I would suggest **red**, **pink**, **purple** and **white** as Oxen's lucky colours for the year 2001.

Use these colours in paints, wall coverings, rugs, drapes and curtains. This will be sure to bring good fortune within the year.

However, Oxen should try not to use green, yellow or brown in 2001, to avoid bad luck.

Lucky Numbers

The lucky numbers for Oxen in 2001 are: **4** and **6**.

Fortune will be much improved by using these lucky numbers whenever possible. For example, if Oxen has a choice, the phone number 264-3466 is better than 257-3379 – because the former contains more fours and sixes, Oxen's two lucky numbers of the year.

Lucky Charm

Feng Shui Masters believe that special objects can be used as a medium between human beings and nature. The fortune of the recipient is greatly improved as the positive wave of energy from nature is passed through the object or 'lucky charm' on to the recipient.

The lucky charm for the Ox in 2001 is a red stone carving with three tangerines, three peaches and three pomegranates as shown below. For the best result, this stone carving should be placed in the west or the north direction of the house.

Chapter Ten

The

Tiger

Years of the Tiger

1914 (4/Feb/14—4/Feb/15)	1962 (4/Feb/62—3/Feb/63)
1926 (4/Feb/26—4/Feb/27)	1974 (4/Feb/74—3/Feb/75)
1938 (4/Feb/38—4/Feb/39)	1986 (4/Feb/86—3/Feb/87)
1950 (4/Feb/50—3/Feb/51)	1998 (4/Feb/98—3/Feb/99)

Distribution of the Stars within the Sign for 2001

Lucky Stars	Unlucky Stars
Heavenly Virtue	Tongues Wag
Star of Blessing	Funeral Robe
Blessing Virtue	Robbery Threat

Lucky Stars

Heavenly Virtue

Virtue was highly appreciated by Confucius, the great Chinese philosopher. The ancient Chinese believed that virtue not only set a good example to others, but provided its own benefits and rewards as well. The Chinese Horoscope has four 'Virtue' Stars, with Heavenly Virtue being the most influential.

The appearance of this Star is definitely a very good omen. It minimizes negative influences from the Unlucky Stars, and bestows a peaceful and joyful year.

Star of Blessing

During Chinese New Year it is customary to decorate the home with a prominent piece of red paper on which the Chinese character 'Blessing' is printed, in hopes of bringing good luck. Similarly, in the Chinese Horoscope the presence of the 'Star of Blessing' is considered to be most lucky.

This Star indicates a very fortunate year. It can even change bad luck to good.

Blessing Virtue

This is another 'Virtue' Star in the Chinese Horoscope. When this Star appears, people will enjoy a year full of blessings from other people. Its message is that it is best to set a good example and be kind to those who have been helpful in the past. By following the practice of 'one good turn deserves another,' blessings will manifest continually.

Unlucky Stars

Tongues Wag

Confucianism endorses the adage 'Silence is Golden.' In ancient Chinese society, gossiping – especially rumour-mongering – was definitely looked down upon.

Should this Star appear within a Sign it is a warning to people to refrain from gossip. Wagging tongues will not only hurt others, but the person who spreads gossip as well.

Funeral Robe

During traditional Chinese funerals, people would wear roughly-tailored yellow hemp clothes as a symbol of their grief, showing they were too overwhelmed with sorrow to worry about finery. Since then these yellow robes have come to symbolize funerals.

The appearance of this Star is not a good omen. It signifies that people need to be alert to potential medical problems among older family members – periodic medical check-ups and, if necessary, effective treatment should be undertaken regularly.

Robbery Threat

Bandits were a nightmare for the peaceful Chinese peasants who were scattered throughout the rural areas that were not well protected by local forces. Their money, crops or even their lives were under continuous threat so that they had to try very hard to protect themselves or they would become helpless victims.

When this Star appears, people should try not to walk alone in the dark streets, and they also should make sure all their windows and doors are locked securely.

General Overview of the Year

This will be a very fortunate and smooth year for the Tiger. Tigers will get the necessary help from others whenever it is needed. However, Tigers should not rely too much on others, as they will see much better achievements if they can take a more aggressive role at work. Their strong leadership will be a very important key to their future success. However, Tigers should try to keep their mouths shut and not talk too much about their business secrets. Tigers will be quite fortunate in money affairs, and they will realize an income from different sources.

Tigers will be in very good shape physically, but they have to watch their personal and home safety.

Tigers will be quite active in social gatherings and will become quite popular among new acquaintances.

```
Career    ****
Money     ***
Health    **
Love      **
```

**** = Very Fortunate/*** = Pretty Good/** = Fair

Career ****

This will be a very fortunate and smooth year for Tigers, so they should try to make good use of this period of time if they want to be successful in the years to come. The most favourable months of the year for the Tiger are the first, second, fifth, ninth and tenth month. Tigers' strong leadership will play a very important role in their success at work during these five months. They must try to keep their mouths shut, however, and not talk too much about their business publicly, or their opportunities will be ruined. Tigers should handle their business with care during the fourth, seventh and the eleventh month. Otherwise, their chances of success in business will be seriously hurt.

Money ***

Tigers will be quite fortunate in money affairs this year. Besides their steady monthly income, Tigers will have other income from different sources. Almost all of their investments will bring good returns throughout the year. Although Tigers will have luck in lottery and gambling, they should not get too greedy. Most important of all, Tigers should not show off too much in order to avoid a robbery or break-in.

The most fortunate months of the year in money affairs for Tigers are the second, fifth, eighth, ninth and the last month of the year.

Health **

Tigers will be in very good shape physically this year. However, they have to mind their personal and home safety. Tigers have to watch their personal safety during the second and seventh month. They have to watch their home safety during the fourth, seventh, tenth and the last month of the year. Over-eating and over-drinking will be the two major setbacks to their health throughout the year. Therefore, it's very important for Tigers to watch their diet constantly.

Love **

Tigers will be quite busily engaged in different kinds of social activities. They will become the prominent figures at these occasions, but they must not talk too much about others or they will be in deep trouble. Avoiding gossip and rumour is the best way for Tigers to be happy and popular throughout the year. Tigers will have better luck in love affairs during the fifth, ninth and the last month of the year. However, they should watch out for the possible intrusion of a stranger between them and their lovers in the sixth month.

According to traditional Chinese astrology, the distributions of the Lucky and Unlucky Stars within a Sign will more or less determine a person's fate in a particular year. Just as the distributions of the Stars change from year to year, however, they also change from month to month. Each Sign's fate for the year and for each month is calculated according to this basic rule.

Monthly In-depth Forecasts
The First Month (4 February – 4 March)

Well begun is half done

This will be a very fortunate and smooth year for Tigers. They are going to have a very good beginning in the first month of the year because of the appearance of so many Lucky Stars within their Sign. They will be very successful if they can make good use of this period of time. A good start will lead them smoothly towards success throughout the year. But first of all, Tigers must set up a chief goal to achieve for themselves, or they will get confused midway through the year.

However, Tigers won't be as fortunate in money affairs this month. They will lose money in gambling. Apart from this, Tigers have to watch out for pick-pockets at the end of the month, or their money and wallets will be gone with the wind.

Tigers should watch their diets, and try not to eat or drink too much this month.

This will be a romantic month for the Tiger. They will be very popular.

The Second Month (5 March – 4 April)

Fine feathers make fine birds

Intelligence and diligence will bring Tigers appreciation and success this month. However, Tigers should not forget about their appearance. Without a proper and pleasant appearance, their chances of success will decrease. Tigers should dress themselves properly for business occasions. Apart from this, Tigers should try to recruit as many capable helpers and partners as possible, because they will prove valuable assets to their success.

The fortune of Tigers will be much improved this month. They will have some luck in lottery and gambling, but Tigers should not get too greedy. Their investments will bring handsome returns.

This month is not a good time for Tigers to make any long journeys. They have to watch their safety and money very carefully on any trips they do have to make. It would be much better if they could rearrange their schedule.

The Third Month (5 April – 4 May)

Speech is silver, but silence is golden

Business will be steady this month, but Tigers should not discuss it too much in public. Their career will be seriously damaged if they can't keep their business secret. A big mouth will be the chief limitation to business developments within this period of time. Tigers should always keep in mind, 'Silence is golden.'

Tigers will be very busy with different social gatherings. They should watch their words carefully during these occasions. They should try not to criticize others, or they will suffer from endless personal disputes in the months to come.

Money affairs will fluctuate frequently over the course of the month, so Tigers should be conservative in handling money matters.

The Fourth Month (5 May – 4 June)

Don't get mad, get even

Tigers will face several cases of unfair treatment this month. In spite of this, they should try to calm down before they make any response. Their anger will only make the situation worse. Tigers should not get mad, but even. Their reasonable and logical protests will bring them a pleasant surprise eventually. Most important of all, Tigers should try to maintain a stable working atmosphere if they don't want any delays or interruptions in their projects. Persuasion will be more effective than force on the road to success this month.

Tigers should watch their home safety carefully this month. They should make sure that the windows and doors of their houses are securely locked to avoid robbery or break-in.

Tigers will become quite emotional during this period, and they should try to relax. It would be a good idea to take a vacation this month.

The Fifth Month (5 June – 6 July)

Fortune favours the brave

Tigers will be very successful in their careers if they are courageous enough to take calculated risks within this month. Their leadership and strong determination will set a very good example to partners and subordinates. Apart from this, Tigers should stand firm against opponents without fear or hesitation. Tigers have enough intelligence and energy to overcome all opposition this month.

If they fall in love, Tigers should not be afraid to show their affection. A bunch of flowers or some small gifts with affectionate notes will be the most suitable keys to opening up the gates of love.

Tigers will see splendid returns from investments this month because of the appearance of some Lucky Stars within their Sign.

The Sixth Month (7 July – 6 August)

The early bird catches the worm

Although the fortune of Tigers will take a bit of a downward turn this month, it will be quite possible for them to achieve their goals if they put in extra effort at work. There will be no short-cuts to success during this period, so Tigers have to fight all the way for themselves. They should keep in mind that only the early bird catches the worm, and any delays will be costly. There will be rumours and gossip flying around; Tigers should not get angry about this because their anger will only make the situation worse.

Tigers should go to the doctor for a check-up or treatment at the first sign of any lung or liver trouble this month. Any delay will be dangerous.

A stranger may try to step in between Tigers and their lovers. They should try their best to handle the situation properly at this very early stage, or the whole thing will become very complicated and get beyond their control eventually.

The Seventh Month (7 August – 6 September)

It is best on the safe side

This is one of the most unfavourable months of the year for Tigers because of the appearance of several Unlucky Stars within the Sign. They will face severe challenges at work, so they should put more time and effort in to managing their work properly. Any mistakes during this period will become the weapons with which their opponents will attack them mercilessly. Tigers should play safe and cover up their weaknesses properly during this period.

Most important of all, Tigers should try to avoid gambling their money in high-risk investments, or they will be big losers. They will probably lose more money than they'd ever anticipated.

Tigers should try not to walk alone in the dark streets at night within this month to avoid robbery or street violence. Apart from this, Tigers should take care of elder family members to make sure that they are getting proper medical care.

The Eighth Month (7 September – 7 October)

Separate the wheat from the chaff

The fortune of Tigers will improve this month, yet they still have to struggle hard for survival in their careers. They will be left far behind their opponents if they can't keep up the pace at the beginning of the month. However, diligence alone cannot guarantee success; the ability to choose the right partners will play an even more important role in this matter. All their effort will be in vain if Tigers fail to find suitable partners to assist them. There will be different opportunities knocking at the door, but not all of them are practical. Tigers must try their best to find the most profitable one and make it their future target if they want to be more successful in the years to come.

Tigers will be confused in romance during this period. They have to consider things objectively again and again before they can make a decision. In other words, they should not jump up to conclusions.

The Ninth Month (8 October – 6 November)

There is always room at the top

This is one of the most favourable months of the year for Tigers, so they should try not to waste their time fooling around or they will end up with nothing at year end. Tigers will probably be promoted during this period if they really try hard at work. They should try to broaden their professional skills if they want to be more successful in the near future. There will be no limits to their success if they keep on upgrading themselves. Tigers should keep in mind that they should not rely on others too much, because they will have better achievements if they can take a more active and aggressive role at work.

Tigers will have unexpected income this month. However, they should not show off too much in order to avoid a robbery or break-in.

Tigers will become active again in social activities this month. They will be quite popular among new acquaintances. They will probably enjoy a close relationship with one of these acquaintances later on.

The Tenth Month (7 November – 6 December)

Eagles don't catch flies

Tigers will be quite productive this month if they work closely with partners. However, they should try to concentrate on their main target only, and leave the minor ones to subordinates. Otherwise, Tigers will end up exhausted by minor details and won't have enough time or energy to manage the major task. Lack of concentration will be the major hurdle to success this month. If Tigers want to have a successful business meeting or seminar, it will be much better if it can be arranged for the beginning of the month.

Tigers should watch out for fire this month. They should check the safety of all electronic devices at the office and at home.

Tigers should not play with fire in romance during this period, or they will surely get burned.

The Eleventh Month (7 December – 4 January)

Lend your money and lose your friends

This is one of the most unfortunate months for Tigers in money affairs. They will lose a lot of money if they don't keep alert to money traps. First of all, Tigers should not get involved in any loans. Debts will become nightmares in the months and years to come if they do so. If someone asks them for money during this period, they should refuse the request politely, because they will have great difficulty getting the money back later on. Worst of all, they will not only lose their money, but their friend, too. Tigers should be cautious about their spending and investments, as in previous months.

Many problems and disputes at work will arise suddenly this month. Tigers must try their best to settle these as soon as possible. Fortunately, if Tigers can handle them properly and promptly they won't cause too much damage.

The relation between Tigers and their lovers will be at a low ebb this month. Tigers should not ignore complaints from their lovers, or they will be very sorry in the near future.

The Twelfth Month (5 January – 3 February)

Many hands make light work

Tigers will enjoy smooth personal and business relations within this month. They will get the necessary assistance from others whenever needed. Just like the old saying goes, 'Many hands make light work.' Tigers will be able to handle their work easily and efficiently together with their partners and subordinates.

This is one of the most fortunate months for Tigers in money matters. They will be able to earn a pretty good income from different sources due to the appearance of several Lucky Stars within their Sign. But they have to take good care of their money and they have to make sure that the windows and doors of their office and house are securely locked to avoid a burglary or break-in. Their major concern this month is not how to earn money, but how to protect it.

Tigers should spend more time with their family members this month. They should pay particular attention to the health and emotional state of elder family members. They will enjoy a sweet family life this month, and this will provide them with an invaluable memory to them in coming years.

The Tigers' romantic life will turn a new page. Whether it will have a happy ending or not is all up to them.

Using Feng Shui to Improve Fortune: Directions, Colours, Numbers and Lucky Charm

The ancient Chinese used the traditional Horoscope to predict their fortune on a yearly basis – they used the art of Feng Shui to improve their luck.

It was their belief that the application of tactical Feng Shui would change their bad luck into good, and make their good luck improve even more.

This same method is still effective in today's modern world.

There are four main elements which I will use in tactical Feng Shui:

◆ Lucky Directions
◆ Lucky Colours
◆ Lucky Numbers
◆ Lucky Charm

This will be a very fortunate and smooth year for Tigers. They will get the necessary assistance from others whenever needed. They will see even better achievements if they can take a more active and aggressive role. Tigers will be very fortunate in money affairs this year. They will have income from different sources. They will be in very good condition physically. Tigers will be quite active and popular in different social activities, but this won't be a romantic year for them.

I would suggest the following Feng Shui tactics to ensure greater success throughout the year.

Lucky Directions

The most favourable directions of the year for Tigers are **East**, **South** and **Northwest**. Tigers should sleep or sit in these directions if they wish to improve their fortune.

To make this procedure very simple, divide the house or room into nine imaginary squares. Then, using a compass, check the exact direction of each square as shown in Figure 10. This will help to ensure that you do not make a mistake with the direction.

N. West	North	N. East
West		East
S. West	South	S. East

Figure 10

Tigers should sit in the relevant directions at work or while studying; this will ensure that their achievements are much greater than the Stars intended. To improve health and achieve a good night's sleep, Tigers should position their bed in the favourable direction shown (Northwest).

However, Tigers should try to keep away from the unfavourable directions of the year; that is, Southeast and Southwest as shown in

Figure 10. The Tiger should try not to sit, work or sleep in these directions, in order to get rid of the negative influences lurking there.

Lucky Colours

According to Chinese tradition, each of the five elements has its own representative colours. Fire is represented by red, pink and purple, Earth by yellow and brown, and so on. As a Feng Shui Master I would suggest **yellow**, **brown**, **blue**, **grey** and **black** as Tigers's lucky colours for the year 2001.

Use these colours in paints, wall coverings, rugs, drapes and curtains. This will be sure to bring good fortune within the year.

However, Tigers should try not to use green or white in 2001, to avoid bad luck.

Lucky Numbers

The lucky numbers for Tigers in 2001 are: **3** and **8**.

Fortune will be much improved by using these lucky numbers whenever possible. For example, if Tigers has a choice, the phone number 238-3368 is better than 246-4799 – because the former contains more three and eights, Tigers's two lucky numbers for the year.

Lucky Charm

Feng Shui Masters believe that special objects can be used as a medium between human beings and nature. The fortune of the recipient is greatly improved as the positive wave of energy from nature is passed through the object or 'lucky charm' on to the recipient.

The lucky charm for the Tiger in 2001 is a pair of running horses made of yellow stone. This pair of horses is running on top of a city wall, with a bow on their left-hand side, as shown below. For the best result, they should be placed in the east or the north-west direction of the house.

Chapter Eleven

兔

The
Rabbit

Years of the Rabbit

1915 (5/Feb/15—4/Feb/16)   1963 (4/Feb/63—4/Feb/64)
1927 (5/Feb/27—4/Feb/28)   1975 (4/Feb/75—4/Feb/76)
1939 (5/Feb/39—4/Feb/40)   1987 (4/Feb/87—3/Feb/88)
1951 (4/Feb/51—4/Feb/52)   1999 (4/Feb/99—3/Feb/00)

Distribution of the Stars within the Sign for 2001

Lucky Stars	Unlucky Stars
None	Dog of Heaven
	Disastrous Threat
	Funeral Guest
	Swallowed Up
	Gaol House

Unlucky Stars

Dog of Heaven

In Chinese mythology a big, fierce dog would come to threaten and eat people who had done bad deeds. Chinese mythology teaches that this creature causes the eclipse of the Sun and Moon, by swallowing either sphere. During eclipses, the people would bang cymbals or other metal objects to scare the dog and make him spit out the Sun or Moon, thus ending the eclipse.

When this Star appears, people need to stand strong and fight their opponents or they will be swallowed up.

Disastrous Threat

This is one of the four 'Threat' Stars in the Chinese Horoscope. Its appearance is a serious warning to people that if they don't take precautions to protect themselves they could face disastrous results.

People should pay more attention to protect their houses as well as their own safety. They should try to keep away from dangers and try not to take any risks. 'Safety first' is the most important rule that they should follow within the year.

Funeral Guest

When attending funerals in ancient China it was customary to wear white as a symbol of sadness and sobriety. Wearing red or other bright colours showed a lack of respect, and was forbidden on such sombre occasions.

This Star's appearance is a very bad omen, indicating the possibility of death among family and friends. Take extra care of older family members or anyone else who might be in danger.

Swallowed Up

The ancient Chinese peasants faced numerous threats to their possessions. Their grain might be swallowed up by birds, their poultry and domestic animals might be swallowed up by wolves and tigers and, in their barns, their stored food might be swallowed up by rats or bandits.

When this Star appears, people have to take good care of their belongings and protect what they have worked hard to earn from other people.

Gaol House

Going through the judicial system was often a nightmare for the ancient Chinese, since their human rights were not well protected by the judicial system. They would rather have died than have to go to prison.

When this Star appears, people will have a tendency to get in trouble with the law. It is best to stay on the straight and narrow and avoid anything that causes trouble. Keep in mind that 'it is better to be a hungry bird in the forest than a well-fed bird in a cage.'

General Overview of the Year

Rabbits will have a pretty rough year because of the appearance of several Unlucky Stars within their Sign. Rabbits should try to keep alert to oncoming dangers, or they might be swallowed up by their opponents. Rabbits must keep in mind that they should never get involved in any illegal activities this year, or they will surely end up in gaol. Fortunately, their struggles will pay off handsomely at year end.

Financially this won't be a fortunate year for Rabbits. They should try to keep away from borrowing.

Rabbits must try to get enough rest and sleep to avoid a sudden physical collapse.

Rabbits should try to calm down in romance, and concentrate only on their careers and money affairs.

Career   **
Money   *
Health   **
Love   *

** = Fair/* = Unsatisfactory

Career **

Rabbits will have to struggle very hard to survive in business this year. They must bolster their determination and put in extra effort at work, because they have no one to rely on but themselves. Fortunately, their long struggles will pay off at the end of the year, but they have to take good care of their hard-earned rewards or all their efforts throughout the year will be taken away from them. Most important of all, Rabbits should never get involved in any illegal activities this year, or they will surely end up in gaol. Rabbits will face a lot of difficulties and challenges during the first, second, fifth, sixth and tenth month. They should put more time and effort in at work during these months. Rabbits will enjoy better luck at work during the third, ninth and eleventh month; they should try to make good use of these months.

Money *

Rabbits won't have too much luck in money affairs this year, therefore they should watch their budgets very carefully. In addition, Rabbits have to keep alert about protecting their money from being stolen. They should be more conservative in handling money matters during the first, second, seventh, tenth and the last month of the year. They will be very sorry if they gamble their money during these months. Most important of all, Rabbits should try not to get involved in any loans within the year, or they will be in deep trouble.

Health **

Since their health will not be terribly good this year, Rabbits should try to watch their diets and get enough rest and sleep before it's too late. They should pay special attention to their health during the first, fifth, eighth, ninth and the last two months of the year. Apart from this, Rabbits must try to keep away from danger and not take any risks when they go out and about during the second and the seventh month.

Love *

This year won't be a romantic one for Rabbits. Actually, they should not spend too much time on love affairs because there are so many other things for them to take care of. They should try to calm down and concentrate only on their careers and money affairs. They will face problems in love during the first, third, fourth, fifth, tenth and the last month of the year. They should try to do something to repair their relationships during these months, or they will find themselves without a lover by the end of the year.

According to traditional Chinese astrology, the distributions of the Lucky and Unlucky Stars within a Sign will more or less determine a person's fate in a particular year. Just as the distributions of the Stars change from year to year, however, they also change from month to month. Each Sign's fate for the year and for each month is calculated according to this basic rule.

Monthly In-depth Forecasts
The First Month (4 February – 4 March)

Bad money drives out good

This is definitely not a fortunate month for Rabbits due to the appearances of several Unlucky Stars within their Sign. Their major concern within this period is money matters. Rabbits should not try to gamble in high-risk investments, or they will lose a lot of money. Apart from this, they should keep an eye out for money traps. There will probably be a sudden drop in sales or clients; at this very early stage, Rabbits must try to prevent the situation from getting any worse.

A stranger will try to step in between Rabbits and their lovers this month. Rabbits will be very sorry if they don't take this matter seriously and try to settle it before it is too late. Just as the old saying goes, 'Bad money drives out good.' Rabbits should not be blinded by over-confidence.

It's time for Rabbits to stick to their guns and do their best to survive. It would be unwise for them to make any major changes at work during this period.

The Second Month (5 March – 4 April)

Curiosity killed the cat

Although the fortune of Rabbits improves a little this month, there are still several career obstacles ahead. Rabbits should concentrate on their own business, and not get involved in other people's. If they do, Rabbits will become the victims in a very complicated business situation. Apart from this, Rabbits must try not to challenge their superiors even if they don't agree with them. It will be much better if they can avoid getting embroiled in rumour or gossip.

Rabbits will have recovered a bit physically this month but they have to watch their personal safety. They should not get too close to dangerous places when out on journeys. If they risk their safety for the sake of satisfying their curiosity, Rabbits will suffer.

The fortune of Rabbits will be going up and down like a roller-coaster within this period, so that it won't be wise for them to try their luck at gambling and investments. However, they don't have to worry about their living because they will enjoy a steady income.

The Third Month (5 April – 4 May)

He who will eat the fruit must climb the tree

This is one of the most favourable months of the year for Rabbits because of the appearance of several Lucky Stars within the Sign. However, Rabbits have to fight hard for themselves because they will have no one else to rely on within this period of time. They have to bolster their determination and put all their effort into work if they want to achieve their goals. If they don't, they will miss out on a very good opportunity to upgrade their careers. Rabbits should try to get enough sleep even though they are working hard for their achievements. A physical collapse will surely cause irreparable damage.

Money matters improve for Rabbits this month. They will see profits from their investments. Nevertheless, they should try not to get involved in any loans.

Rabbits will become quite passionate during this period. They should keep calm and try not to let their passions run away with them. If there's a proposal of love, they should consider it carefully. They should not jump to conclusions during this period because they will lose their wits in the heat of their passion.

The Fourth Month (5 May – 4 June)

Hope for the best, prepare for the worst

The fortune of Rabbits will fluctuate from time to time throughout the month, so they should keep alert to possible troubles and obstacles, and settle them before things get out of control. A good plan for the rest of the year will help Rabbits to overcome adversity smoothly. Rabbits must keep in mind that they should hope for the best and prepare for the worst in the coming months. Rabbits will tend to get involved in illegal activities this month. They must try to cut out all their connections with any illegal parties, or they will surely end up in gaol sooner or later.

It's wise for Rabbits to pay all their bills as soon as possible. Apart from this, they should save more money for the rainy days to come. In other words, they may have a lot of unexpected expenses in the months to come.

Rabbits should try their best to avoid a serious quarrel with their lovers during this period, or they will face a broken relationship in the near future.

The Fifth Month (5 June – 6 July)

The walls have ears

Rabbits will not only face many difficulties at work, but also numerous personal disputes and conflicts within the month. Therefore, they must work hard and try to keep a low profile for their own self-preservation and for the future success of their career. They must watch their words carefully this month. Under no circumstances should Rabbits ever speak behind the backs of their superiors or colleagues. Just as the old saying goes, 'The walls have ears.' Rabbits can hardly expect others to keep their secrets for them. Furthermore, Rabbits should try to uncover hidden enemies as soon as possible, and then keep away from them beneath a friendly disguise. An attack from behind will prove a critical blow to their careers.

Rabbits will be troubled by rumour and gossip about their romance during this period. They should keep their eyes wide open and keep their mouths shut to make sure that their words don't make the situation even worse.

Rabbits should try to watch their safety in water in the middle of the month. They shouldn't try to risk their lives in the pursuit of fun right now.

The Sixth Month (7 July – 6 August)

There is always a first time

Rabbits have to face certain new career changes this month. They should try to adapt themselves to these new changes as soon as possible, or they will be left behind. Now comes the time for renovation at work. Rabbits should not hesitate to take the necessary action. They should not worry too much, because there is always a first time. Once they get used to the innovations, they will be in a much better career position.

Rabbits will probably fall in love during this period. They should not be shy about expressing their true feelings and affection. They will have a nice surprise if they ask for a date.

This is one of the Rabbit's most fortunate months for money matters. Rabbits will enjoy unexpected income during this period. But they will be deeply disappointed if they gamble.

The Seventh Month (7 August – 6 September)

There are no great losses without some gain

The fortune of Rabbits will fluctuate this month, so they should keep their eyes wide open to the ever-changing situation. The beginning of the month seems to be quite fortunate for Rabbits in money matters, but things will fall off suddenly towards the end of the month. Therefore, Rabbits should not be too greedy with investments even though they may make some gains early in the month.

The same thing pertains to their careers this month, so Rabbits should try to curb their ambition even though they may be quite successful at the beginning of the month. They must carry out their projects step by step to avoid a sudden fall. This month is a good time for Rabbits to think about new development if they want to be able to quit their job in the near future.

Rabbits don't have too much to worry about regarding their health this month. However, they have to drive with extreme care, especially near month's end.

The Eighth Month (7 September – 7 October)

God helps those who help themselves

Rabbits may become frustrated under the continuous pressure of a heavy workload right now. However they should not give up, because if they do, all their efforts and achievements will be swallowed up by their opponents. Actually, Rabbits will be able to get their pay-off for their long struggling at work very soon. Therefore, they should stand up firmly and refuse to give up under any circumstances. God helps those who help themselves.

This is a very good time for Rabbits to take a vacation. They will return much refreshed, and this will benefit their work and health. Rabbits should at least get enough sleep and rest, even if it's impossible for them to take a vacation this month.

Rabbits have to watch financial problems very carefully in the months to come. Gambling will lead only to total destruction, so they'd better forget all about it during this period.

The Ninth Month (8 October – 6 November)

Change for the better is a full-time job

Rabbits will become quite creative and productive this month, so they should try to make use of this opportunity to improve their work. They are quite capable of removing obstacles on their way to success during this period. It's probable that a very important business agreement can be reached at month's end. The major concern of the month for Rabbits is to forge better communications with their clients. This will ensure greater success in the months to come. However, they should keep in mind that 'Change for the better is a full-time job', and should keep up their efforts for the rest of the year, not just for this month only.

If Rabbits wish to buy property, this is a suitable time. However, the value of the property should not go beyond their financial capability.

Rabbits will be in a pretty good shape physically this month. They will, however, be troubled by toothache and infections in the mouth and throat, so they should try to clean their mouths properly and keep away from spicy and raw foods.

The Tenth Month (7 November – 6 December)

Cheats never prosper

Rabbits must cut all connections with illegal parties this month, or they will surely be punished by law. All illegal activities should be given up at once, or Rabbits will end up very sorry indeed. Apart from this, Rabbits should play by the rules when handling their business, because any dirty tricks will bring only negative results sooner or later. Honesty is the best policy if they want to keep up good and harmonious business relations with their clients. However, they should not reveal any business secrets.

The fortune of Rabbits in money affairs will be not as good as last month. In any case, Rabbits needn't worry too much about this as long as they don't get involved in any kinds of loans. Rabbits should keep their eyes wide open for money traps. Nor should they be deceived by a false friend.

Rabbits should not cheat on their lovers, because cheats never prosper, especially during this period of time. However, it's the proper time for them to show their true feelings to their lovers; a mutual understanding will probably be reached as a result.

The Eleventh Month (7 December – 4 January)

A little of everything, and nothing will be achieved

Rabbits will be very busy at work this month. They should try to concentrate only on major tasks, however, or all their efforts will be in vain. Just as the old saying goes, 'A little of everything, and nothing will be achieved.' Rabbits should draw up a good schedule to keep their work organized, or their projects won't be carried out efficiently. This is not a good time for Rabbits to change jobs; even if they're really keen to do so they'll have to wait until next year.

Rabbits should not be too picky about meeting new (or old) friends, or they will be left isolated. Their loneliness during this period is their own fault. Prejudice will be the major hurdle in social and love affairs.

Rabbits should not try their luck at gambling or they will be disappointed. Apart from this they should watch their budgets, because they tend to over-expend this month.

The Twelfth Month (5 January – 3 February)

You never miss the water until the well runs dry

This is one of the most unfavourable months of the year for Rabbits, so they must keep alert to a sudden collapse in their career or in money matters. It would be a great pity if Rabbits lost all their hard-earned rewards at this final post. Rabbits will run out of cash this month if they haven't saved enough over the past few months. They will probably spend more money than they could ever have anticipated. Just as the old saying goes, 'You never miss the water until the well runs dry.'

Fortunately, Rabbits won't have too much trouble handling their daily work. However, they should not forget to keep up good and harmonious relations with clients, or they will be defeated by their opponents in the near future.

Rabbits will be hospitalized for exhaustion if they don't get enough rest and sleep as suggested in previous months. Fortunately, it won't be too late for them if they start to keep fit now.

Using Feng Shui to Improve Fortune: Directions, Colours, Numbers and Lucky Charm

The ancient Chinese used the traditional Horoscope to predict their fortune on a yearly basis – they used the art of Feng Shui to improve their luck.

It was their belief that the application of tactical Feng Shui would change their bad luck into good, and make their good luck improve even more.

This same method is still effective in today's modern world.

There are four main elements which I will use in tactical Feng Shui:

◆ Lucky Directions
◆ Lucky Colours
◆ Lucky Numbers
◆ Lucky Charm

This will be a pretty rough year for Rabbits. They should keep alert to watch out for continuous challenges, or they will be swallowed up by their opponents. They have no one to rely on except themselves. This won't be a fortunate year in money matters for Rabbits. They should also watch their health and safety closely. Rabbits should try to restrain themselves from sex and pleasure, and try to concentrate more on career and money affairs.

I would suggest applying the following Feng Shui tactics to improve luck so Rabbits don't have to worry too much about their fate within the year.

Lucky Directions

The most favourable directions for Rabbits are **South, Northwest** and **North**. Rabbits should sleep or sit in these directions if they wish to improve their fortune.

To make this procedure very simple, divide the house or room into nine imaginary squares. Then, using a compass, check the exact direction of each square as shown in Figure 11. This will help to ensure that you do not make a mistake with the direction.

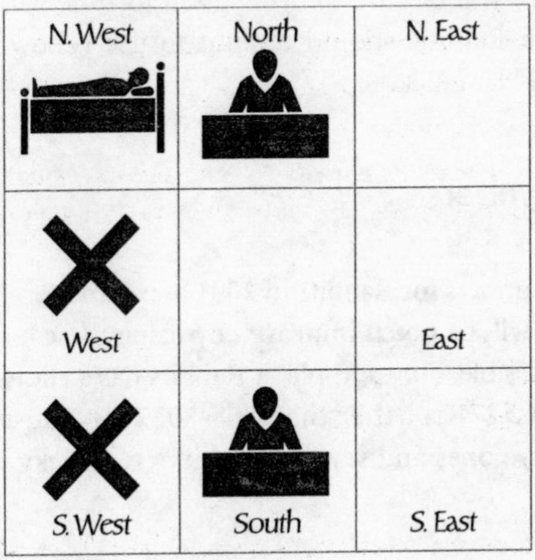

Figure 11

Rabbits should sit in the relevant directions at work or while studying; this will ensure that their achievements are much greater than the Stars intended. To improve health and achieve a good night's sleep, Rabbits should position the bed in the favourable direction shown (Northwest).

However, Rabbits should try to keep away from the unfavourable directions of the year; that is, Southwest and West as shown in Figure 11. Rabbits should try not to sit, work or sleep in these directions, so as to get rid of the negative influences lurking there.

Lucky Colours

According to Chinese tradition, each of the five elements has its own representative colours. Fire is represented by red, pink and purple, Earth by yellow and brown, and so on. As a Feng Shui Master I would suggest **blue**, **grey**, **black** and **white** as Rabbits's lucky colours for the year 2001.

Use these colours in paints, wall coverings, rugs, drapes and curtains. This will be sure to bring good fortune within the year.

However, Rabbits should try not to use yellow or green in 2001, to avoid bad luck.

Lucky Numbers

The lucky numbers for Rabbits in 2001 are: **1** and **7**.

Fortune will be much improved by using these lucky numbers whenever possible. For example, if Rabbits has a choice, the phone number 217-7271 is better than 268-8022 – because the former contains more ones and sevens, Rabbits's two lucky numbers for the year.

Lucky Charm

Feng Shui Masters believe that special objects can be used as a medium between human beings and nature. The fortune of the recipient is greatly improved as the positive wave of energy from nature is passed through the object or 'lucky charm' on to the recipient.

The lucky charm for the Rabbit in 2001 is a black stone carving of a turtle coming out of water and carrying a lotus flower on its back, as shown below. For the best result, this stone carving should be placed in the north or northwest direction of the house.

Chapter Twelve

The

Dragon

Years of the Dragon

1904 (5/Feb/04—3/Feb/05)   1952 (5/Feb/52—3/Feb/53)
1916 (5/Feb/16—3/Feb/17)   1964 (5/Feb/64—3/Feb/65)
1928 (5/Feb/28—3/Feb/29)   1976 (5/Feb/76—3/Feb/77)
1940 (5/Feb/40—3/Feb/41)   1988 (4/Feb/88—3/Feb/89)

Distribution of the Stars within the Sign for 2001

Lucky Star   **Unlucky Stars**

Heavenly Happiness   Isolated Living
Yearly Threat
Heavenly Threat
Illness Spell

Lucky Star

Heavenly Happiness

The Chinese have always considered marriage to be one of the greatest blessings in life. It not only brings the joys of family life, but also helps to perpetuate the family, hopefully for generations to come. Such a gift is considered to be heaven-sent. This Star symbolizes marital happiness and is highly regarded in the Chinese Horoscope.

The presence of this Star signifies romance, a healing of broken relationships, and possibly even marriage before the year is out.

Unlucky Stars

Isolated Living

Living alone without the care and attentions of family members was very much against the Chinese tradition. Only those who had committed wrong-doings were isolated and deserted.

The appearance of this Star is not a good omen. To maintain other people's support and friendship, try to be more open, outgoing and friendly.

Yearly Threat

The ancient Chinese believed that malevolent spirits brought dangers and problems into their daily lives. The Star 'Yearly Threat' was one of these. Its appearance is a bad omen.

When this Star appears, people need to improve relations with others, especially with lovers and spouses, to avoid endless arguments and quarrels.

Heavenly Threat

The ancient Chinese believed that malevolent spirits brought dangers and problems into their daily lives. Of these, 'Heavenly Threat' was considered to be the most dangerous of all, and able to cause serious damage.

The appearance of this Star is a warning to be more careful. Watch out for potential dangers and traps. Follow a conservative, defensive strategy.

Illness Spell

Chinese magical spells were created by Taoist priests, who would write special symbols in red ink or blood on pieces of yellow cloth or paper.

In ancient China, staying healthy was a constant struggle due to the generally poor state of medicine and the living conditions in the villages. When someone became sick it was believed to have been caused by an evil 'Illness Spell' which had entered their home.

When this Star appears people should protect themselves and their family by being extra careful about diet and hygiene.

General Overview of the Year

Although this won't be a very productive year for Dragons, they will enjoy a happy and easy life. Their personal and business relations will be much improved this year, and this will contribute to their success. However, Dragons must keep their eyes open to avoid money traps, or they will be seriously hurt. Dragons should not hesitate to ask for professional advice from experts about money matters whenever needed during this year. Dragons should not expect too much from gambling or investments because their luck won't be good at all this year.

Dragons have to watch their safety when they go fishing or swimming.

This will be a romantic year for Dragons, yet they should try to avoid over-indulgence.

```
Career   ***
Money    **
Health   *
Love     ***
```

*** = Pretty Good/** = Fair/* = Unsatisfactory

Career ***

Dragons will become quite popular among new and old friends this year, and this will be a very good time for them to improve their personal and business relationships. Their popularity will prove to be a big help to their future success. Their main concern this year is not their business but their health and safety, because there will not be too much for them to worry about at work within this period of time. Dragons will have better business opportunities during the first two months, the fourth, eighth, and eleventh month. They should try to make good use of these months if they wish to have a more successful year. Most important of all, Dragons have to keep a careful eye on traps in business and money matters during the third, fifth and eleventh month. If they should fall prey to any of these traps, they should not hesitate to ask for professional advice from experts.

Money **

Financially this won't be a fortunate or profitable year for Dragons. They should not expect too much from gambling and investments because their luck won't be good. They will have a steady income, however, enough for a comfortable living. This means Dragons do not have to worry about their money as long as they are not too greedy. Since there will be several money traps ahead, Dragons should keep alert and try not to let their greediness blind them, or they will be the big losers.

Health *

Dragons will not be in good condition physically this year, so they have to try their best to mind their health. Their indulgence in sex, alcohol and drugs will seriously hurt not only their health but their careers as well. It would be much better for Dragons to keep away from all these temptations. They have to take particular care of themselves during the third, fifth, eighth, ninth and tenth month. Apart from this, Dragons have to mind their safety around water when they go fishing or swimming, especially during the fourth and seventh month.

Love ***

Dragons will have splendid romantic experiences this year, yet they should try to restrain their passion and should never let them run riot. Otherwise there will be endless trouble in the years to come. Dragons will have better luck in love during the first, third, fourth, eighth and the eleventh month. Although Dragons will be very popular among new acquaintances, they should not ignore their old companions, especially during the fifth month, or they'll become somewhat isolated.

According to traditional Chinese astrology, the distributions of the Lucky and Unlucky Stars within a Sign will more or less determine a person's fate in a particular year. Just as the distributions of the Stars change from year to year, however, they also change from month to month. Each Sign's fate for the year and for each month is calculated according to this basic rule.

Monthly In-depth Forecasts
The First Month (4 February – 4 March)

Love makes the world go round

Although Dragons will be quite busy at work this month, they will also be very active at different social occasions. They should try to improve their personal relationships at these kinds of gatherings. If possible, Dragons should try to bring more joy and fun to the people around them; this will bring them a very nice surprise sooner or later. This will be a very romantic month for Dragons, but they have to try not to indulge themselves too much in sex or alcohol, or they will spoil this wonderful period of time.

There will be several opportunities knocking at the door this month. Dragons should try to carry out new projects now, while they have a good chance of success. A compromise with their opponents, rather than confrontation, will make them more successful at work. Dragons should try to reach a mutual understanding with clients during this period.

Dragons will be quite healthy at the beginning of the month, but they will be bothered by minor pains towards the end of the month. Their main concern for this month is their diet. They should try to avoid over-eating or over-drinking.

Dragons will have luck in lottery and gambling. They should not get too ambitious, however, since their luck will turn bad at the end of the month.

The Second Month (5 March – 4 April)

Business before pleasure

Dragons will have a very busy schedule this month and their workload will be quite heavy. They should try their best to finish their work as soon as possible without any delays, or their opponents will make use of this chance to beat them. Under these circumstances, the old saying 'Business before pleasure', should be their motto of the month. There will be disputes among colleagues; Dragons should try to settle these at the earliest stage, or the situation will get out of control in the months to come.

Dragons will be quite busy attending different social activities, as they did the last month. They should not let this take up too much of their time, however, or they will miss several business opportunities.

Dragons will be quite emotional this month. Unless they can control themselves they will scare away not only their colleagues, but their lovers too.

The Third Month (5 April – 4 May)

Waste not, want not

This is one of the most unfortunate months of the year in money matters for Dragons, due to the appearance of several Unlucky Stars within their Sign. They tend to spend more and more money in unusual ways, so they should watch their budget carefully. Dragons must never let their expenses outstretch their incomes, or they will be in deep trouble. 'Waste not, want not': Dragons should keep this motto in mind during the first half of the month.

The love affairs of Dragons will be splendid during this period. However, they should try to restrain their sex drive to avoid making serious mistakes. This is not a good time for Dragons to make any important decisions about romance or marriage, because their minds will not be as clear as usual.

Dragons should watch out for careless mistakes at work. Any mistakes now will bring trouble in the near future.

The Fourth Month (5 May – 4 June)

It takes two to make a bargain

The fortune of Dragons will improve this month, so they should try to make use of this period of time to achieve their goals. Actually, this is a very good bargaining month for them. They can be very successful by negotiating and bargaining. However, they should be more flexible in dealing with opponents or there will be no agreements reached at all, which will deal a serious blow to their careers. Some good news from overseas will probably come in the middle of the month. They should try to respond at once if they don't want a very good chance to slip through their fingers.

Love is a wondrous thing to Dragons this month. They should not play with fire, however, or they will get burned sooner or later.

Dragons should mind their safety in water. They have to take the necessary precautions when fishing or swimming.

The Fifth Month (5 June – 6 July)

A fool may give wise man counsel

This will be quite a confusing period of time for Dragons, and they won't know what to do or where to go. It would be best for them to ask the advice of experts whenever needed. Actually, they should be humble enough to take advice from different kinds of people. The suggestions of ordinary people may spark new ideas for Dragons right now.

Dragons will be quite popular among new acquaintances, yet they should not ignore their old companions or they will end up very sorry very soon. Apart from this, Dragons should be very careful when making jokes.

The fortune of Dragons in money matters will go up and down like a roller-coaster, so they should not risk their money in gambling or investments. Apart from this, they should try not to get involved in loans.

The Sixth Month (7 July – 6 August)

One bad apple spoils the whole barrel

This is one of the most unfavourable months of the year for Dragons, so they should try to quash possible disputes and troubles before they get out of control. Internal disputes will cause severe career damage. It would be much better to detect the source of these problems and eliminate them as soon as possible. Dragons should not be too kind to trouble-makers, because one bad apple spoils the whole barrel. This is definitely not a good time for Dragons to start new projects, as they will face numerous objections and difficulties if they do so.

Dragons should watch their budget carefully to make sure that there won't be any financial problems. They should try to get rid of unprofitable projects, or they will get deeper and deeper in debt.

Dragons tend to be influenced by false friends this month. They should try to keep away from these false friends, or their future will suffer serious damage.

The Seventh Month (7 August – 6 September)

You can't tell a book by its cover

Although internal disputes and problems will dissolve this month, Dragons still won't have an easy time. They tend to be easily cheated during this period of time, so they should keep their eyes wide open to watch out for dirty tricks. As the old saying goes, 'You can't tell a book by its cover.' Dragons should try not to judge people by appearances. If they do, Dragons will be the big losers in terms of their career and money matters. Dragons should also be more objective when handling their daily work.

In love affairs, Dragons will be easily cheated by beautiful appearances this month. They should try not to be so naïve, so as to avoid serious heartbreak.

Fortunately, the health of Dragons is improving. However, they must bear in mind that they should never ignore water safety, especially at the beginning of the month.

The Eighth Month (7 September – 7 October)

Good seed makes a good crop

Just as the old saying goes, 'Good seed makes a good crop' – a good selection of partners and projects will help Dragons to be more successful at work this month. However, a bad choice will spoil their opportunities. Therefore, their success or failure during this time is all up to themselves. Diligence and harmonious relationships will be the two good seeds that will produce a good harvest at the end of the year.

There will be a breakthrough in romance this month; Dragons should try to cultivate this precious seed with their care and affection. If not, this seed will dry up very soon.

This will be a profitable month for Dragons if they can choose their investments carefully. Apart from this, Dragons will receive a small amount of unexpected income at the middle of the month.

The Ninth Month (8 October – 6 November)

Old habits die hard

This month is one of the most unfavourable for Dragons. The major handicap to success during this period will be their own bad habits. But, as the old saying goes, 'Old habits die hard' – it will be almost impossible for Dragons to cut them out totally. However, they should at least try to do as much as they can. Old habits such as staying late at work, being disorganized, or heavy drinking and smoking will hurt not only their careers but their personal life too. If they can get rid of their old habits bit by bit now, it will be the beginning of a new life.

This is not a good time to buy property or luxury items, or Dragons will be very sorry in the months to come. Apart from this, Dragons should take care of their wallets when in crowded places.

Dragons must try to keep away from strange or foreign foods when on their travels, or they will suffer very much as a result. They may enjoy a short romance on their journeys, but it's only a short dream and they should not expect too much.

The Tenth Month (7 November – 6 December)

The darkest hour is just before dawn

Dragons should try not to give up their work under the strain of their long struggles since the beginning of the year, because there will be important breakthroughs in the months to come. They should keep optimistic even though they are under a very heavy workload at this time. Apart from this, their positive attitude will excite the enthusiasm of fellow-workers to fight against the hardships they all face. Others may invite Dragons to take part in new business ventures, but they should turn them all down for the time being.

Dragons should try to maintain a constant connection with their lovers even if they cannot be together physically. If not, some unexpected changes may arise.

Dragons are at the edge of exhaustion this month, so it's very important for them to relax before it is too late.

The Eleventh Month (7 December – 4 January)

Where bees are, there is honey

Finally there are career breakthroughs after long struggling, so Dragons should try their best to collect their rewards during this period of time. However, it's time for Dragons to find new targets for themselves. Dragons should be as sensitive as the bees in looking for honey, and as diligent as the bees in collecting their honey. Most important of all, Dragons should work closely together with their fellow-workers, as the bees working as a team. Failure to do these things will result in a very different scenario.

Dragons will enjoy a very romantic period this month. However, they should not over-indulge or they will miss several business opportunities. There will be some rumours flying about concerning their romance, but they should not care too much if they haven't done anything wrong.

Money matters will change for the better because of the appearance of several Lucky Stars within the Sign. They will profit from investments in property and stocks. Now's a good time for them to start a new business venture or investment.

The Twelfth Month (5 January – 3 February)

East, West, home's best

Dragons will be able to release themselves from the heavy burden of their workload and to enjoy life during this period. It would be wise for them to take a vacation this month. This is precisely what they really deserve, and what they really need. If a vacation is impossible, Dragons should try to spend more time with family. This sweet family life will provide Dragons with unforgettable memories in the years to come.

There will be some older relatives coming to visit from overseas. Dragons should try to avoid over-eating and over-drinking during these pleasant occasions. If they over-indulge, they will be very sorry very soon. Dragons will be in high spirits during this period of time, but they must try to keep away from drugs and alcohol.

Dragons may face money problems if they keep on spending without a second thought. They should try to pay all their bills if possible. The major concern this month is to try to keep away from any loans or debts, or a financial nightmare will arise in the years to come.

Using Feng Shui to Improve Fortune: Directions, Colours, Numbers and Lucky Charm

The ancient Chinese used the traditional Horoscope to predict their fortune on a yearly basis – they used the art of Feng Shui to improve their luck.

It was their belief that the application of tactical Feng Shui would change their bad luck into good, and make their good luck improve even more.

This same method is still effective in today's modern world.

There are four main elements which I will use in tactical Feng Shui:

◆ Lucky Directions
◆ Lucky Colours
◆ Lucky Numbers
◆ Lucky Charm

Although this won't be a very productive year for Dragons, they will enjoy a happy and easy life. Their main concern for the year is to keep their eyes wide open and avoid traps in business and money matters. Dragons should not expect too much from gambling or investments because their luck won't be too good this year. Dragons should try to protect themselves from different kinds of infections. Besides this, they should try to keep away from water. Fortunately this will be a very romantic year for Dragons, yet they should try to restrain themselves from over-indulgence.

I would suggest applying the following Feng Shui tactics to improve Dragons' luck so they don't have to worry too much about their fate within the year.

Lucky Directions

The most favourable directions for Dragons are **Southeast**, **West** and **North**. Dragons should sleep or sit in these directions if they wish to improve their fortune.

To make this procedure very simple, divide the house or room into nine imaginary squares. Then, using a compass, check the exact direction of each square as shown in Figure 12. This will help to ensure that you do not make a mistake with the direction.

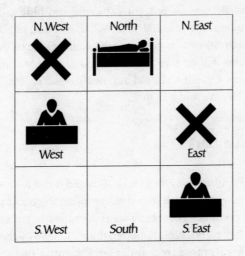

Figure 12

Dragons should sit in the relevant directions at work or while studying; this will ensure that their achievements are much greater than the Stars intended. To improve health and achieve a good night's sleep, Dragons should position the bed in the favourable direction shown (North).

However, Dragons should try to keep away from the unfavourable directions of the year; that is, East and Northwest as shown in Figure 12. The Dragon should try not to sit, work or sleep in these directions, in order to get rid of the negative influences lurking there.

Lucky Colours

According to Chinese tradition, each of the five elements has its own representative colours. Fire is represented by red, pink and purple, Earth by yellow and brown, and so on. As a Feng Shui Master I would suggest **red**, **pink**, **purple** and **blue** as Dragons's lucky colours for the year 2001.

Use these colours in paints, wall coverings, rugs, drapes and curtains. This will be sure to bring good fortune within the year.

However, Dragons should try not to use yellow, brown or green in 2001, to avoid bad luck.

Lucky Numbers

The lucky numbers for Dragons in 2001 are: **2** and **6**.

Fortune will be much improved by using these lucky numbers whenever possible. For example, if Dragons has a choice, the phone number 266-8266 is better than 211-3461 – because the former contains more twos and sixes, Dragons's two lucky numbers for the year.

Lucky Charm

Feng Shui Masters believe that special objects can be used as a medium between human beings and nature. The fortune of the recipient is greatly improved as the positive wave of energy from nature is passed through the object or 'lucky charm' on to the recipient.

The lucky charm for the Dragon in 2001 is a pair of monkeys sitting on a gold ingot with a pearl on their heads and a bat resting on their chests as shown below. For the best result, they should be placed in the southeast or the north direction of the house.

Day-by-day Analysis of Luck

Do the right thing at the right time every day

The charts that appear on pages 210 – 313 relate particularly to the art of perfect timing. The principle of daily forecasting or Chinese 'date-choosing' stems from the belief that there is a time and a place for everything. The ancient Chinese believed that certain things were particularly suited to certain days. The calculation and application of this becomes the framework for date-choosing.

Through their observations, the ancient Chinese realized that different kinds of plants need different climates to grow, and that they had to follow nature's rules if they were to have good harvest. For them, it therefore followed that a single day cannot be suitable for *all* tasks and activities. Thus, people have to choose a suitable day to do their jobs if they want to achieve good results.

The calculation involved in date-choosing can seem complicated, but fortunately there are some traditional Feng Shui rules that make things easier. The calculation is based mainly on the distribution of the different Stars on different days. Because this distribution changes from day to day, the suitable activities also change accordingly.

Format

The format of these forecast charts (which run from 1 January 2001 to 31 December 2001) is as follows:

The first two columns list the **Date** and **Day of the week**.

The third column lists the **Favourable Activities** for that day. Days highlighted in ★ indicate a very fortunate day; those with a • indicate a fair-to-middling day; those with ♦ indicate an unlucky day. Try not to schedule important activities for unlucky days; however, if you cannot avoid doing a certain job on an unlucky day, choose the **Lucky Hours** of that day (column four). This alternative is sometimes quite effective. Neither are all hours suitable, even on a generally very fortunate day. Choosing the lucky hours for a task or project can add to the effect of a fortuitous day, while less lucky hours can undermine this effect.

The ancient Chinese believed there were good directions and bad directions, and that these changed on a daily basis. The three most important were the **Direction of Happiness** (column five), the **Direction of Wealth** (column six) and the **Direction of Opportunity** (column seven).

The Direction of Happiness is an auspicious pointer for seating plans at weddings, birthday parties, etc., to ensure happiness for all participants.

If looking for good investments or good income, sitting in the Direction of Wealth on a given day will enhance your efforts.

If looking for promotion or a breakthrough in your career or in your studies, sitting in the Direction of Opportunity for a given day will foster success.

Most important of all, there will be some brief forecasts for individual Signs under the chart, so that readers can know what they are going to face during that particular period of time when using the charts. This will prove to be a very helpful supplement to the 'Monthly In-depth Forecasts' of the Signs in previous chapters.

Explanations

The 32 activities listed are divided into seven categories:

- ◆ Spiritual Rites
- ◆ Social Interactions
- ◆ Out and About
- ◆ Commercial Activities
- ◆ Cleaning
- ◆ Household Activities
- ◆ Outdoor Pursuits

Spiritual Rites

(1) Worship

The ancient Chinese used to worship different kinds of gods and spirits. For instance, they would worship the Gods of heaven, the Gods of nature, and the honorable dead such as the historical figures and their ancestors. In order to purify themselves before the gods or honourable dead, they would not eat any meat nor take any wine for a period of time, and would take a bath shortly before the worship ceremony. According to the Chinese tradition, there were certain days especially suitable for worship.

(2) Blessing

The ancient Chinese would go to the temples and ask the monks there to perform the blessing ceremony for them when they were experiencing troubles over a period of time. They hoped that their luck would change from bad to good as a result. In order to have a better result, they would choose a suitable day for blessing.

There is a big difference between 'Blessing' and 'Worship'. The former refers to the blessing of the living people, while the latter refers to the memorial ceremony for the gods or the honourable dead.

(3) Burial

The ancient Chinese believed that whether the newly dead were buried properly or not would have strong influences over the fate of their descendants. As a result, they would sincerely ask the Feng Shui Masters to choose a good place and good timing to bury their newly dead family member. They considered that the burial timing must be right, or the Feng Shui of the grave would be minimized.

According to the Chinese tradition, there were some days especially suitable for burial of the dead. Not only the living descendants would be benefited, but also the buried dead could rest peacefully in the grave as a result.

Social Interactions
(4) Engagement

The procedures of an ancient Chinese marriage were very complicated and tediously long. From engagement to wedding would take months or even years. The parents of the young couple would insist that both engagement and wedding should take place on lucky days to ensure a happy ending and a fruitful marriage with many offspring. During the engagement, the parents of both families had to exchange gifts as a sign of commitment to one another.

(5) Wedding

The meaning of marriage in the ancient China was quite different from that of nowadays. The ancient Chinese marriage was considered to be the tool of reproduction so that the family could keep on growing from generation to generation. The emphasis of an ancient marriage was on reproduction rather than on true love between the young man and woman.

The parents would therefore choose a lucky day for the wedding ceremony of their youngsters, to ensure as many descendants as possible. Date-choosing for wedding has remained a primary concern in Chinese society over the centuries.

(6) Social Gathering

Friendship and harmonious relationships were highly appreciated in ancient China. People would choose a lucky day to meet their new and old friends. They would clean themselves and prepare gifts before the meeting to show their sincerity. They believed that there would be a happy gathering, mutual understanding and agreement as a result.

This can apply to formal and informal social gatherings of different natures, such as birthday parties, fund-raising events, exhibitions and conferences in the modern society.

(7) Start Learning

The ancient Chinese would study very hard to pass the Civil Examination, because they could change their social status from the common class to the ruling class after they performed well. Parents would urge their youngsters to go to school at an early age. The 'Start Learning' ceremony was one of the most important events in a person's life, because not too many people would have the chance to receive an education. The ceremony was very serious and would be performed only on the lucky day, to ensure the success in the future examination.

Nowadays this can also apply to starting different kinds of lessons, such as in driving, dancing, singing and so on.

Out and About

(8) Moving

The ancient Chinese were very reluctant to move house, either to move to a new home or a new town, because they were afraid to give up the old and start all over in a new place. In order to increase their confidence, they would choose a lucky day for moving. They believed that this would make their new lives easier and smoother.

(9) Travelling

The ancient Chinese used to bind themselves to their cultivated lands because all their wealth, property and relatives were closely connected with their lands. As a result, they were very reluctant to travel. Besides which, the traffic systems were not well developed at the time, so that travelling would be quite uncomfortable and dangerous. If they had to travel, they would choose a lucky day to start their journey. They hoped that a good beginning would bring a good ending.

Commercial Activities

(10) Grand Opening

The ancient Chinese merchants would choose a very lucky day for the grand opening of their shops in order to have a good beginning of their business. Usually, firecrackers and the lion dance would be used during the ceremony to bring good luck to the shop.

Nowadays, the moment of ribbon-cutting and champagne-toasting should take place at the lucky hour of the lucky day, to ensure a successful venture.

(11) Signing Contracts

Even in ancient China it was the norm for contracts to be drawn up and signed to confirm any business or legal transactions. In order to avoid argument and conflicts in the future, the parties involved would choose a lucky day to sign these contracts.

This can apply to the signing of different kinds of commercial and legal documents in the modern world.

(12) Trading

Commercial activities were not common in ancient China, nor were well appreciated. However, different kinds of trading would take place in different ways, such as trading of crops, domestic animals, fields and houses. Both the buyer and the seller would choose a lucky day for trading in order to bring about the greatest possible mutual benefit.

This can apply to the trading of different kinds of business in the modern world. People can earn more profit if they pick a lucky day for their trading, according to traditional Chinese beliefs.

[13] Money Collecting

The ancient Chinese considered that money in the market was similar to fish in the river: neither was easy to catch. Just as the fishermen would wait for the right tide to catch fish, the Chinese would choose the right timing to collect money. If they chose the wrong time to do so, they then would not only have difficulties in collecting money, but also would have difficulties keeping hold of it.

Cleaning
[14] House Cleaning

The ancient Chinese considered that the house of a family was equivalent to the body of a person. Both should be kept clean at all times, or disease and bad luck would ensue.

People would go to the doctor and clear up the accumulated toxic deposits inside the body when they were sick. In much the same way, people would choose a lucky day to clean their homes thoroughly when they had been experiencing bad luck over a period of time. They hoped that their bad luck would be swept away with the dirt from their homes.

[15] Bathing

The meaning of 'bath' in the Chinese date-choosing was quite different from that of the daily bath in the modern world. In ancient times, the Chinese would clean themselves thoroughly before important ceremonies to show their purity and sincerity. They would carefully choose a suitable day to take this ritual bath. In addition, some would keep to a vegetarian diet for a period of time in order to purify their bodies completely inside and out.

If they had been experiencing bad luck for a period of time, they would add some kind of herbs to the bath water to wash away the bad luck.

(16) Hair Cutting

The ancient Chinese had a very strong feeling about their hair because it was regarded as a symbol of their ego. Without a proper hairstyle, it was felt they would lose all sense of self and self-esteem. History tells us that thousands and thousands of Chinese were killed by a new ruler between 1644 and 1645 simply because they refused to cut their hair.

The ancient Chinese believed that to cut hair on lucky days for this activity would bring good luck.

(17) Tailoring

The ancient Chinese of the common class had few clothes because they couldn't afford them. They would have clothes made for them only for very special occasions, such as weddings, birthdays and New Year's Day. They would choose a lucky day to have fittings at the tailor because they believed that this would bring good luck to them.

Household Activities

(18) Bed Set-Up

The main entrance, stove and sleeping bed are considered the three essential factors in Feng Shui studies. Therefore, to set up a bed in the proper place at the proper time in a new house is a prime concern of the Feng Shui Master. If it is done properly, the person who sleeps in the bed will enjoy good sleep and, consequently, good health.

If people wanted to get a new bed but the Feng Shui Master was not available to help them, they would choose a lucky day from the calendar to do so.

(19) Stove Set-Up

The stove (cooker) is considered important because it is closely related to the health of the whole family. According to Feng Shui theory, if the stove is set up in the wrong place of the kitchen, the food prepared in it will spoil the health of the family members.

(20) Door Fixing

The ancient Chinese used to pay special attention to the main entrance of their homes because of security and Feng Shui reasons. They considered that a pair of sturdy doors at the main entrance, acting as the main gate to guard them from being attacked by robbers and gangsters, were of primary importance. They also considered that if the door at the main entrance opened in the right direction to let the good *Chi* (positive energy) flow into the house, the Feng Shui of that house would be greatly enhanced. No matter the reasons, they would choose a lucky day to fix the door at their main entrance.

(21) Crack Refilling

The ancient Chinese considered that the small cracks and large holes that appear in walls and anywhere else in the home or workplace should be filled in as soon as possible. This stemmed in part from practical reasons: if there were no holes, then no rats, snakes or poisonous insects or animals could live there. The work usually involved using cement and different herbs to fill up the cracks and holes. They would choose a suitable day to do this kind of work, but not necessarily a very lucky day.

(22) Wall Decorating

The ancient Chinese considered the wall of a house to be as important as the face of a human being. If there were some cracks or dirt on the wall, that meant the owner lost 'face'. They would hire workers to repair and redecorate in a suitable fashion. They believed that their luck would be changed after that.

This can apply to decorating with paint or wallpaper. It is also applicable to the practice of tearing down old walls and building new ones.

(23) Construction

The ancient Chinese would break the ground of a site at the beginning of each new construction. In order to please the guardian spirits of the earth, they would kill a rooster and pig as sacrifices to the spirits as part of the ground-braking ceremony. The ceremony had to take place at the lucky hour of the lucky day to ensure the safety of the new structure. The ancient Chinese deeply believed that to break the ground at the wrong time would lead to many problems and accidents during construction.

(24) Ditching

The ancient Chinese villagers used to dig ditches in and out of their cultivated-lands and houses for irrigation and washing. They would carefully choose the right direction in which to dig the ditches, at the right time, in order to let the good Chi flow in together with the water. According to Feng Shui theory, the water should flow in from the good direction and flow out towards the bad direction.

This can apply to any piping or plumbing work in the modern houses. The building of a pond or swimming pool is another modern-day example.

(25) Passage Fixing

The passages of a house were considered to be as important as the blood vessels of a human body. Therefore, good maintenance of the passages were necessary in order to keep good Feng Shui. If there was any damage, then it would be fitting to repair it as soon as possible. The ancient Chinese believed that to change a rough passage into a smooth one would change their luck from bad to good. People would choose a lucky day for fixing passages in and out of their homes.

(26) Nursery Set-Up

To have more offspring in order to increase the family was the prime concern of the ancient Chinese. Therefore, they would be very serious about choosing a lucky day to set up a nursery room for their baby. They believed that a good nursery set-up would bring a healthy baby with good fortune.

This can also be applied to the set-up of a cot or Moses basket for a newborn baby.

Outdoor Pursuits

(27) Hunting

Hunting was not very common in ancient China because it was the privilege of the nobility. But gradually the common people would go hunting on a much smaller scale on some special occasions. In order to ensure a safe and productive hunt, they would choose a lucky day to go hunting.

(28) Capturing

According to Chinese tradition, there was a difference between hunting and catching. Hunting involved killings with weapons, while catching referred to catching animals and birds alive with nets or traps. The former was the privilege of the nobility, while the latter was a common practice among the lower classes.

(29) Planting

The ancient Chinese paid special attention to planting because agriculture was their major source of income. Besides the plantation of major crops, they would have some other crops to supplement their income. They believed that the harvest of any crop would be determined by the day on which it was planted. If they didn't choose the right timing, then their harvest would be spoiled.

This can also apply to the planting of flowers and fruit trees on a smaller scale. The plants will grow much better if a suitable day for planting is chosen according to the classic Chinese calendar.

(30) Animal Acquiring

The ancient Chinese farmers would raise some animals and fowl such as pigs, sheep, ducks and chickens to supplement their incomes. Because infections were very common among these kinds of domestic creatures, the farmers had to be very cautious about raising them. When they wanted to bring in some new animals, they would choose a lucky day to do so. They believed that an unlucky day would bring in bad luck together with the animals, especially in the form of infections and disease.

This can apply to the buying of the small domestic pets, such as cats, dogs, rabbits, gerbils, canaries, budgerigars, etc. To buy these pets or to accept them as gifts on a lucky day is believed to ensure their healthy growth, and also a close relationship between the animals and the owners.

(31) Fishing

Chinese fishermen used to go out to the open sea for fishing with sampans or junks. These small wooden boats were not strong enough for the rough sea. Any accidents could happen suddenly. They might end up losing their boats or even their lives.

In order to avoid these kinds of tragedies, the fishermen would set up strict rules to be followed among themselves; choosing a lucky day for fishing was one of them. They believed that this would bring them back safely with abundance of fish.

This also applies to angling in any form.

(32) Net Weaving

Fishermen used nets to catch fish in the water, while 'capturers' used nets to trap animals in the forest. Therefore, nets were very important in the ancient Chinese villages. Both the fishermen and capturers would take good care of their nets. They would choose a lucky day to prepare new nets or to repair the old ones.

This can apply to the preparation of objects that are similar to nets, such as fences, drapes and curtains.

Date	Day	Favourable Activities
Jan 1	Mon	• Hair Cutting, Bathing
2	Tue	★ Blessing, Construction, Travelling, Wedding, Social Gathering, Moving, Trading, Burial
3	Wed	★ Grand Opening, Trading, Construction, Planting, Tailoring, Social Gathering, Travelling, Signing Contracts
4	Thu	• Passage Fixing, Wall Decorating
5	Fri	★ Blessing, Signing Contracts, Animal Acquiring, Wedding, Engagement, Trading, Construction
6	Sat	★ Construction, Stove Set-up, Engagement, Trading, Signing Contracts
7	Sun	★ Blessing, Planting, Moving, Construction, Engagement, Travelling, Wedding, Burial

★ Lucky Day   • Ordinary Day   ◆ Unlucky Day

Lucky Hours			Direction of Happiness	Direction of Wealth	Direction of Opportunity
23-01 01-03 03-05 07-09 13-15 15-17			NE	SE	NE
23-01 01-03 03-05 05-07 15-17 17-19			NW	SE	N
23-01 05-07 17-19			SW	W	W
03-05 13-15			S	W	NW
01-03 05-07 09-11 15-17 17-19			SE	N	NE
23-01 03-05 11-13 15-17			NE	N	SW
01-03 03-05 11-13 15-17 17-19			NW	E	SW

Dog – You better watch out for your money, and better to keep it in a safe place. *Mouse* – Don't forget to show your care and affection to your loved ones. *Dragon* – No pain, no gain. You have to try harder for your future success. *Pig* – Don't let your personal matters mess up your business. *Sheep* – You have to go step by step to avoid a sudden big fall. *Snake* – You will have some unexpected income, but easy come, easy go.

Date	Day	Favourable Activities
Jan 8	Mon	◆ Unlucky Day Not suitable for important activities
9	Tue	★ Worship, Hair Cutting, House Cleaning, Grand Opening, Money Collecting, Burial
10	Wed	★ Moving, Start Learning, Trading, Wedding, Grand Opening, Travelling, Engagement, Burial
11	Thu	◆ Unlucky Day Not suitable for important activities
12	Fri	★ Blessing, Nursery Set-up, Construction, Ditching, Social Gathering, Grand Opening, Tailoring, Start Learning
13	Sat	• Worship, Net Weaving, Burial
14	Sun	• Worship, Signing Contracts

★ Lucky Day   • Ordinary Day   ◆ Unlucky Day

Lucky Hours	Direction of Happiness	Direction of Wealth	Direction of Opportunity
03-05 05-07 09-11 11-13 15-17	SW	E	S
23-01 01-03 05-07 07-09 09-11 17-19	S	S	E
23-01 01-03 03-05 07-09 09-11 15-17	SE	S	SE
01-03 03-05 05-07 09-11	NE	SE	NE
23-01 01-03 03-05 05-07	NW	SE	SW
23-01 01-03 09-11 17-19 21-23	SW	W	W
23-01 09-11 11-13 17-19 21-23	S	W	NW

Tiger – Don't try your luck with lotteries or gambling, or you will be very sorry. *Rooster* – It's time to build up a better business relationship now. *Monkey* – You will be in pretty good shape, but don't try any drugs. *Rabbit* – Your romance is going to turn a new page. *Horse* – You will be quite fortunate in money affairs. *Ox* – Watch your diet very carefully.

Date	Day	Favourable Activities
Jan 15	Mon	★ Bed Set-up, Stove Set-up, Moving, Engagement, Bathing, House Cleaning
16	Tue	★ Blessing, Engagement, Grand Opening, Net Weaving, Start Learning, Money Collecting
17	Wed	• Worship, Wall Decorating
18	Thu	★ Blessing, Animal Acquiring, Construction, Moving, Signing Contracts, Money Collecting, Trading
19	Fri	★ Bed Set-up, Hunting, Capturing, Bathing, Hair Cutting
20	Sat	◆ Unlucky Day Not suitable for important activities
21	Sun	★ Grand Opening, Travelling, Stove Set-up, Moving, Construction, Burial

★ Lucky Day   • Ordinary Day   ◆ Unlucky Day

Lucky Hours			Direction of Happiness	Direction of Wealth	Direction of Opportunity
01-03 05-07 07-09 09-11 11-13			SE	N	NE
23-01 03-05 05-07 11-13			NE	N	SW
01-03 03-05 07-09 09-11 11-13 21-23			NW	E	NE
01-03 03-05 09-11 11-13			SW	E	NE
01-03 03-05 05-07 09-11 21-23			S	S	E
23-01 03-05 09-11 11-13			SE	S	E
23-01 01-03 07-09 09-11 15-17 17-19			NE	SE	SW

Sheep – Calm down and think again. Don't make a hasty decision now. *Dragon* – You are going to have a very romantic week. *Pig* – Business before pleasure. *Monkey* – Be modest, don't try to be too aggressive. *Ox* – You will be full of energy and confidence at work. *Dog* – Better watch quality control now.

Date	Day	Favourable Activities
Jan 22	Mon	★ Wedding, Signing Contracts, Trading, Travelling, Grand Opening, Engagement, Construction, Burial
23	Tue	◆ Unlucky Day Not suitable for important activities
24˙	Wed	Chinese New Year
25	Thu	● Worship, Bathing, Tailoring, Bed Set-up
26	Fri	● Worship, Tailoring
27	Sat	★ Signing Contracts, Engagement, Wedding, Money Collecting, Trading, Construction, Planting, Burial
28	Sun	★ Worship, Grand Opening, Travelling, Stove Set-up, Bed Set-up, Burial

★ Lucky Day   ● Ordinary Day   ◆ Unlucky Day

Lucky Hours			Direction of Happiness	Direction of Wealth	Direction of Opportunity
23-01 01-03 03-05 07-09 15-17 17-19			NW	SE	SW
23-01 03-05 05-07 09-11 15-17 17-19 21-23			SW	W	W
01-03 03-05 11-13 17-19 21-23			S	W	W
01-03 05-07 07-09 09-11 15-17 17-19			SE	N	NE
23-01 03-05 05-07 09-11 15-17 17-19			NE	N	N
01-03 03-05 05-07 07-09			NW	E	NE
03-05 05-07 09-11 11-13			SW	E	NE

Horse – It's time to look for your next target. *Rabbit* – Don't complain about your heavy schedule, because it will pay off handsomely. *Snake* – The harder you work, the luckier you get. *Tiger* – Don't expect too much in love. *Rooster* – You have to try to keep to a tight budget, or you will be very sorry. *Mouse* – Keep your eyes open for money traps.

Date	Day	Favourable Activities
Jan 29	Mon	• Capturing, Burial
30	Tue	★ Social Gathering, Money Collecting, Construction, Moving, Engagement, Signing Contracts, Trading
31	Wed	★ Worship, Hair Cutting, Bathing, House Cleaning, Hunting
Feb 1	Thu	◆ Unlucky Day Not suitable for important activities
2	Fri	★ Worship, Start Learning, Grand Opening, Wedding, Door Fixing, Construction, Burial
3	Sat	◆ Unlucky Day Not suitable for important activities
4	Sun	• Start Learning, Crack Refilling

★ Lucky Day   • Ordinary Day   ◆ Unlucky Day

Lucky Hours			Direction of Happiness	Direction of Wealth	Direction of Opportunity
01-03 03-05 05-07 09-11 17-19 21-23			S	S	E
23-01 05-07 07-09 09-11 15-17			SE	S	SE
01-03 03-05 17-19			E	SE	SW
23-01 03-05 05-07 15-17 21-23			NW	SE	SW
23-01 01-03 09-11 15-17 17-19 21-23			SW	W	W
01-03 11-13 17-19 21-23			S	W	NW
01-03 05-07 11-13 13-15			SE	N	NE

Monkey – Be modest at work, and don't exceed your abilities. *Ox* – Your dreams may come true if you have really tried your best. *Tiger* – It's time to think about renovations. *Dog* – Watch out for hypocrites. *Sheep* – Keep away from cliffs, high walls and long ladders to avoid a big fall. *Mouse* – It's not a good time for gambling.

Date	Day	Favourable Activities
Feb 5	Mon	◆ Unlucky Day Not suitable for important activities
6	Tue	● Worship, Start Learning, Bathing, Bed Set-up
7	Wed	● Worship, Net Weaving, Crack Refilling
8	Thu	★ Engagement, Signing Contracts, Trading, Tailoring, Animal Acquiring, Burial
9	Fri	★ Trading, Travelling, House Cleaning, Hair Cutting, Engagement, Signing Contracts
10	Sat	● Blessing, Social Gathering, Tailoring, Net Weaving
11	Sun	● Passage Fixing

★ Lucky Day   ● Ordinary Day   ◆ Unlucky Day

Lucky Hours			Direction of Happiness	Direction of Wealth	Direction of Opportunity
23-01 03-05 05-07 11-13 13-15			NE	N	SW
01-03 13-15 17-19			NW	E	NE
01-03 03-05 05-07 11-13 13-15			SW	E	NE
01-03 03-05 05-07 13-15 19-21			S	S	E
23-01 03-05 05-07 19-21			SE	S	E
23-01 01-03 03-05 07-09 13-15 17-19			NE	SE	SW
23-01 01-03 17-19 19-21			NW	SE	N

Snake – You must take adequate rest and sleep to avoid a sudden physical collapse. *Horse* – The early bird catches the worm, so wake up and work early. *Rabbit* – It's better to be safe than sorry. *Dragon* – Although you will have some luck in lottery and gambling, you should not be too greedy. *Rooster* – Honesty is the best policy in your love affairs. *Dog* – Things are beautiful if you love them.

Date	Day	Favourable Activities
Feb 12	Mon	★ Grand Opening, Wedding, Door Fixing, Trading, Construction, Engagement, Bed Set-up, Burial
13	Tue	★ Worship, Blessing, Animal Acquiring, Travelling, Moving, Construction, Burial
14	Wed	◆ Unlucky Day Not suitable for important activities
15	Thu	★ Worship, Bathing, Hair Cutting, House Cleaning, Fishing, Burial
16	Fri	• Start Learning
17	Sat	◆ Unlucky Day Not suitable for important activities
18	Sun	◆ Unlucky Day Not suitable for important activities

★ Lucky Day   • Ordinary Day   ◆ Unlucky Day

Lucky Hours	Direction of Happiness	Direction of Wealth	Direction of Opportunity
09-11 11-13 17-19 19-21	SW	W	NW
09-11 11-13 13-15 17-19	S	W	NW
01-03 07-09 09-11 13-15	SE	N	SW
23-01 07-09 09-11 11-13 13-15	NE	N	SW
01-03 11-13 13-15	NW	E	SW
01-03 03-05 05-07 11-13 13-15 19-21	SW	E	S
23-01 01-03 03-05 05-07 07-09 09-11 13-15	S	S	E

Tiger – You will be quite popular during this period. *Mouse* – You have to watch your personal hygiene very carefully. *Dragon* – There will be several opportunities knocking at your door. *Dog* – You will be more persuasive, and it might help you fight for a very important contract. *Ox* – A little knowledge is a dangerous thing. *Sheep* – Try to keep an optimistic and positive attitude at work.

Date	Day	Favourable Activities
Feb 19	Mon	• Bed Set-up, Stove Set-up
20	Tue	• Social Gathering, Animal Acquiring, Trading, Signing Contracts
21	Wed	★ Engagement, Signing Contracts, Social Gathering, Trading, Hair Cutting, Bathing
22	Thu	★ Worship, Blessing, Wedding, Grand Opening, Moving, Travelling, Construction, Burial
23	Fri	• Worship, Passage Fixing
24	Sat	★ Grand Opening, Trading, Engagement, Moving, Travelling, Construction, Wedding, Burial
25	Sun	• Worship, Social Gathering, Capturing, Fishing

★ Lucky Day   • Ordinary Day   ◆ Unlucky Day

Lucky Hours			Direction of Happiness	Direction of Wealth	Direction of Opportunity
23-01 01-03 07-09 09-11 17-19 19-21			SE	S	E
03-05 07-09 13-15 17-19 19-21			NE	SE	NE
03-05 05-07 13-15 19-21			NW	SE	SW
09-11 17-19			SW	W	W
01-03 09-11 11-13 13-15 17-19 19-21			SW	W	W
05-07 09-11 13-15 17-19			SE	N	SW
03-05 05-07 09-11 11-13 13-15			NE	N	SW

Rabbit – Watch out, a stranger may try to step in on your romance.
Snake – Don't let your personal life get entangled with your career.
Pig – Be more considerate to the people around you, and you will be handsomely rewarded. *Monkey* – It never rains, but it pours. *Horse* – You will be able to get good returns from your investments. *Rooster* – Don't eat or drink too much at social gatherings.

Date	Day	Favourable Activities
Feb 26	Mon	◆ Unlucky Day Not suitable for important activities
27	Tue	• Worship, Blessing
28	Wed	★ Worship, Blessing, Start Learning, Construction, Grand Opening, Trading, Signing Contracts, Burial
Mar 1	Thu	◆ Unlucky Day Not suitable for important activities
2	Fri	• Worship, Start Learning, Travelling, Social Gathering
3	Sat	• Worship
4	Sun	★ Social Gathering, Engagement, Signing Contracts, Trading, Animal Acquiring, Burial

★ Lucky Day   • Ordinary Day   ◆ Unlucky Day

Lucky Hours	Direction of Happiness	Direction of Wealth	Direction of Opportunity
01-03 07-09 09-11 11-13 13-15	NW	E	SW
03-05 07-09 09-11 11-13	SW	E	NE
03-05 05-07 09-11 13-15 19-21	S	S	E
03-05 05-07 07-09 11-13 19-21	SE	S	E
23-01 01-03 03-05 07-09 13-15	NE	SE	NE
23-01 01-03 03-05 05-07 17-19	NW	SE	N
23-01 05-07 11-13 17-19	SW	W	W

Ox – You will have a wonderful time with your loved ones. *Horse* – Sensibility and diligence will be the two wings of your success; you can't fly high without them. *Monkey* – Keep away from fire, or you will get burned. *Dog* – It's the right time for you to take a vacation. *Mouse* – Try to restrain your desires and don't let them get out of control. *Tiger* – Well begun is half done.

Date	Day	Favourable Activities
Mar 5	Mon	★ Construction, Moving, Grand Opening, Wedding, Bed Set-up, Planting, Travelling, Burial
6	Tue	• House Cleaning, Bathing, Hair Cutting, Travelling
7	Wed	• Engagement, Tailoring, Animal Acquiring
8	Thu	• Worship, Stove Set-up, Wall Decorating, Passage Fixing
9	Fri	★ Trading, Wedding, Signing Contracts, Tailoring, Construction, Start Learning, Animal Acquiring
10	Sat	• Worship, Bathing, House Cleaning, Hunting
11	Sun	◆ Unlucky Day Not suitable for important activities

★ Lucky Day   • Ordinary Day   ◆ Unlucky Day

Lucky Hours	Direction of Happiness	Direction of Wealth	Direction of Opportunity
03-05 11-13 13-15	S	W	NW
01-03 05-07 09-11 13-15 15-17	SE	N	NE
23-01 03-05 11-13 13-15 15-17	NE	N	SW
01-03 03-05 11-13 13-15 15-17	NW	E	SW
03-05 05-07 09-11 11-13 15-17	SW	E	S
23-01 01-03 05-07 07-09 09-11 13-15	S	S	E
23-01 01-03 03-05 07-09 09-11 15-17	SE	S	SE

Pig – Better try to settle personal disputes as soon as possible. *Rooster* – If you want something done well, do it yourself. *Sheep* – You have to cut out unnecessary expenses or you will be in deep trouble very soon. *Rabbit* – Don't make drastic changes in business. *Snake* – Watch out for attacks from hidden enemies. *Dragon* – Love makes the world go around.

Date	Day	Favourable Activities
Mar 12	Mon	★ Travelling, Trading, Construction, Bed Set-up, Wedding, Moving, Grand Opening, Burial
13	Tue	◆ Unlucky Day Not suitable for important activities
14	Wed	• Net Weaving, Capturing
15	Thu	★ Wedding, Nursery Set-up, Moving, Travelling, Construction, Ditching, Animal Acquiring, Engagement
16	Fri	★ Signing Contracts, Tailoring, Wall Decorating, Net Weaving, Trading
17	Sat	• Worship, Bathing, House Cleaning, Hunting
18	Sun	• House Cleaning, Hair Cutting, Bathing, Travelling

★ Lucky Day   • Ordinary Day   ◆ Unlucky Day

Lucky Hours			Direction of Happiness	Direction of Wealth	Direction of Opportunity
01-03	03-05	05-07	NE	SE	NE
09-11	13-15				
23-01	01-03	03-05	NW	SE	SW
05-07	13-15				
23-01	01-03	09-11	SW	W	W
19-21					
23-01	09-11	11-13	S	W	NW
01-03	05-07	07-09	SE	N	NE
09-11	11-13	13-15			
23-01	03-05	05-07	NE	N	SW
11-13	13-15				
01-03	03-05	07-09	NW	E	NE
09-11	11-13	13-15			

Sheep – You tend to be moody this week, so try to control your emotions. *Tiger* – Dress up and make yourself look nice; this will help you be more successful. *Ox* – You must try to sort out misunderstandings with your loved ones. *Rabbit* – If you want to survive, you must be more flexible. *Rabbit* – Never try to challenge your superiors. *Mouse* – The sea never refuses water. *Horse* – Relax, and don't exhaust yourself.

Date	Day	Favourable Activities
Mar 19	Mon	◆ Unlucky Day Not suitable for important activities
20	Tue	• Worship, Passage Fixing, Wall Decorating
21	Wed	★ Worship, Grand Opening, Trading, Wedding, Construction, Signing Contracts, Burial
22	Thu	★ Worship, Start Learning, House Cleaning, Bathing, Capturing
23	Fri	◆ Unlucky Day Not suitable for important activities
24	Sat	★ Worship, Fishing, Capturing, Hunting, Tailoring
25	Sun	◆ Unlucky Day Not suitable for important activities

★ Lucky Day   • Ordinary Day   ◆ Unlucky Day

Lucky Hours			Direction of Happiness	Direction of Wealth	Direction of Opportunity
01-03	03-05	09-11	SW	E	NE
11-13	13-15	19-21			
01-03	03-05	05-07	S	S	E
09-11	13-15				
23-01	03-05	05-07	SE	S	E
09-11	11-13	19-21			
23-01	01-03	07-09	NE	SE	SW
09-11	13-15	15-17			
23-01	01-03	03-05	NW	SE	SW
07-09	15-17				
23-01	03-05	05-07	SW	W	W
09-11	15-17	19-21			
01-03	03-05	11-13	S	W	W
13-15	19-21				

Dragon – Business before pleasure. *Monkey* – You must be very conservative in handling your money affairs. *Dog* – Don't count your chickens before they are hatched. *Rooster* – You must try to reach a mutual understanding with loved ones. *Pig* – You will be quite fortunate in money affairs. *Pig* – Pay special attention to the health and safety of your children at home. *Snake* – Don't lose confidence.

Date	Day	Favourable Activities
Mar. 26	Mon	• Hair Cutting, Capturing, Net Weaving, Fishing
27	Tue	★ Start Learning, Engagement, Wedding, Moving, Grand Opening, Hair Cutting, Travelling, Construction
28	Wed	★ Signing Contracts, Trading, Planting, Tailoring, Money Collecting
29	Thu	• Social Gathering, Travelling, Trading, Signing Contracts
30	Fri	• Travelling, Hair Cutting, House Cleaning
31	Sat	★ Blessing, Grand Opening, Money Collecting, Trading, Social Gathering, Signing Contracts
Apr 1	Sun	• Worship, Wall Decorating, Passage Fixing

★ Lucky Day   • Ordinary Day   ◆ Unlucky Day

Lucky Hours			Direction of Happiness	Direction of Wealth	Direction of Opportunity
01-03 05-07 07-09 09-11 15-17			SE	N	NE
23-01 03-05 05-07 09-11 15-17			NE	N	N
01-03 03-05 05-07 07-09			NW	E	NE
03-05 05-07 09-11 11-13 19-21			SW	E	NE
01-03 03-05 05-07 09-11			S	S	E
23-01 05-07 07-09 09-11 15-17 19-21			SE	S	SE
01-03 03-05 13-15			NE	SE	SW

Horse – Try to finish your work as quickly as possible; any delays will be dangerous. *Tiger* – It's time to find a capable partner for yourself if you want to be more successful. *Rooster* – Don't put all your eggs in one basket. *Pig* – You will be quite creative and capable at work. *Pig* – Try to save more money for the rainy days to come. *Ox* – Never leave your children home alone.

Date	Day	Favourable Activities
Apr 2	Mon	★ Worship, Blessing, Social Gathering, Money Collecting, Tailoring
3	Tue	● Travelling, House Cleaning, Net Weaving, Fishing
4	Wed	◆ Unlucky Day Not suitable for important activities
5	Thu	◆ Unlucky Day Not suitable for important activities
6	Fri	◆ Unlucky Day Not suitable for important activities
7	Sat	★ Wedding, Signing Contracts, Grand Opening, Trading, Constructions, Start Learning, Travelling
8	Sun	● Worship, Capturing, Fishing, Animal Acquiring

★ Lucky Day   ● Ordinary Day   ◆ Unlucky Day

Lucky Hours	Direction of Happiness	Direction of Wealth	Direction of Opportunity
23-01 03-05 05-07 15-17 19-21	NW	SE	SW
23-01 01-03 09-11 13-15 15-17 19-21	SW	W	W
01-03 11-13 13-15	S	W	NW
01-03 05-07 11-13 13-15 15-17	SE	N	NE
23-01 03-05 05-07 11-13 13-15 15-17	NE	N	SW
01-03 13-15 15-17 17-19	NW	E	NE
01-03 03-05 05-07 09-11 11-13 15-17	SW	E	NE

Sheep – Don't throw pearls before swine. *Rabbit* – Don't risk your safety just to satisfy your curiosity. *Mouse* – Keep away from raw food and seafood. *Snake* – It's time to go in on a joint venture in business. *Snake* – Faith and enthusiasm will be the two important factors in your success. *Dog* – You should spend more time with your family this week. *Monkey* – It's a good time to take a vacation.

Date	Day	Favourable Activities
Apr 9	Mon	★ Grand Opening, Construction, Travelling, Trading, Moving, Nursery Set-up, Wedding, Start Learning
10	Tue	• Crack Refilling
11	Wed	• Worship
12	Thu	◆ Unlucky Day Not suitable for important activities
13	Fri	• Worship
14	Sat	• Passage Fixing, Wall Decorating
15	Sun	• House Cleaning, Bathing, Animal Acquiring, Door Fixing

★ Lucky Day   • Ordinary Day   ◆ Unlucky Day

Lucky Hours	Direction of Happiness	Direction of Wealth	Direction of Opportunity
01-03 03-05 05-07 13-15	S	S	E
23-01 03-05 05-07	SE	S	E
23-01 01-03 03-05 07-09 13-15 17-19	NE	SE	SW
23-01 01-03 15-17 17-19	NW	SE	N
09-11 11-13 15-17 17-19	SW	W	NW
09-11 11-13 13-15 17-19	S	W	NW
01-03 07-09 09-11 13-15 15-17	SE	N	SW

Dragon – Try to handle your business with extreme care, because any careless mistakes within this period will be costly. *Pig* – The unexpected always happens, so you must keep alert. *Ox* – Do right and fear no man. *Tiger* – Keep your eyes open and your mouth shut. *Horse* – Watch your budget; a penny saved is a penny earned. *Rooster* – Don't expect too much in love affairs.

Date	Day	Favourable Activities
Apr 16	Mon	★ Worship, Bathing, Wedding, Hair Cutting, Net Weaving, Fishing, Animal Acquiring, Burial
17	Tue	◆ Unlucky Day Not suitable for important activities
18	Wed	◆ Unlucky Day Not suitable for important activities
19	Thu	★ Engagement, Wedding, Travelling, Signing Contracts, Grand Opening, Construction, Trading, Burial
20	Fri	• Worship, Capturing, Hunting, Animal Acquiring
21	Sat	★ Grand Opening, Ditching, Signing Contracts, Moving, Planting, Travelling, Construction, Trading
22	Sun	• Worship, Wall Decorating

★ Lucky Day   • Ordinary Day   ◆ Unlucky Day

Lucky Hours	Direction of Happiness	Direction of Wealth	Direction of Opportunity
23-01 07-09 09-11 11-13 13-15 15-17	NE	N	SW
01-03 11-13 13-15 15-17	NW	E	SW
01-03 03-05 05-07 11-13 13-15	SW	E	S
23-01 01-03 03-05 05-07 07-09 09-11 13-15	S	S	E
23-01 01-03 07-09 09-11 15-17 17-19	SE	S	E
03-05 07-09 13-15 17-19	NE	SE	NE
03-05 05-07 13-15 15-17	NW	SE	SW

Dog – One bad apple spoils the whole barrel. *Sheep* – You can rely on no one but yourself to solve your problems. *Mouse* – A bird never flew on one wing. *Rabbit* – Never get involved in any loans this month. *Snake* – Watch your road safety; walk and drive with extreme care. *Monkey* – A compromise will be much better than a confrontation right now.

Date	Day	Favourable Activities
Apr 23	Mon	• Worship
24	Tue	★ Planting, Money Collecting, Grand Opening, Construction, Trading, Moving, Engagement, Wedding
25	Wed	• Worship, Grand Opening, Social Gathering, Net Weaving
26	Thu	• Net Weaving, Hair Cutting
27	Fri	• Worship, Bathing, House Cleaning, Animal Acquiring
28	Sat	★ House Cleaning, Capturing, Hair Cutting, Bathing, Burial
29	Sun	◆ Unlucky Day Not suitable for important activities

★ Lucky Day   • Ordinary Day   ◆ Unlucky Day

Lucky Hours	Direction of Happiness	Direction of Wealth	Direction of Opportunity
09-11　15-17　17-19	SW	W	W
01-03　09-11　11-13 13-15　17-19	S	W	W
05-07　09-11　13-15 15-17　17-19	SE	N	SW
03-05　05-07　09-11 11-13　13-15　15-17	NE	N	SW
01-03　07-09　09-11 11-13　13-15　15-17	NW	E	SW
03-05　07-09　09-11 11-13	SW	E	NE
03-05　05-07　09-11 13-15	S	S	E

Ox – You have to keep your eyes open to watch out for money traps. *Horse* – Try to resist sexual temptation within this period or you will get burned. *Monkey* – Try to relax to avoid a nervous breakdown. *Snake* – Unity is strength; try to form a powerful alliance. *Pig* – Watch out for a pick-pocket or burglary. *Pig* – Don't ignore your loved ones or you will be very sorry.

Date	Day	Favourable Activities
Apr 30	Mon	◆ Unlucky Day Not suitable for important activities
May 1	Tue	★ Blessing, Start Learning, Social Gathering, Animal Acquiring, Trading, Grand Opening, Travelling
2	Wed	• Capturing, Fishing, Animal Acquiring, Money Collecting
3	Thu	★ Start Learning, Moving, Construction, Travelling, Social Gathering, Trading, Grand Opening, Engagement
4	Fri	◆ Unlucky Day Not suitable for important activities
5	Sat	• Wall Decorating, Tailoring
6	Sun	• Net Weaving

★ Lucky Day   • Ordinary Day   ◆ Unlucky Day

Lucky Hours			Direction of Happiness	Direction of Wealth	Direction of Opportunity
03-05 05-07 07-09 11-13			SE	S	E
23-01 01-03 03-05 07-09 13-15 15-17			NE	SE	NE
23-01 01-03 03-05 05-07 15-17 17-19			NW	SE	N
23-01 05-07 11-13 17-19			SW	W	W
03-05 11-13 13-15			S	W	NW
01-03 05-07 09-11 13-15 15-17 17-19			SE	N	NE
23-01 03-05 11-13 13-15 15-17			NE	N	SW

Rooster – You have to try to upgrade your equipment and business data now. *Sheep* – Be patient or you will suffer a fall in front of your opponents. *Tiger* – Don't get mad, get even. *Rabbit* – Try to settle any legal actions as soon as possible. *Dragon* – You should watch your safety in water. *Mouse* – There's no smoke without fire. *Dog* – Health is wealth, so you should mind your personal hygiene.

Date	Day	Favourable Activities
May 7	Mon	★ Worship, Travelling, Planting, Wedding, Moving, Construction, House Cleaning, Burial
8	Tue	• Worship, Nursery Set-up
9	Wed	• Worship, Bathing, Passage Fixing, House Cleaning
10	Thu	★ Construction, Start Learning, Grand Opening, Trading, Travelling, Wedding, Moving, Burial
11	Fri	★ Wedding, Hair Cutting, Bathing, Construction, Capturing, Bed Set-up
12	Sat	◆ Unlucky Day Not suitable for important activities
13	Sun	★ Planting, Moving, Construction, Travelling, Bed Set-up, Tailoring

★ Lucky Day   • Ordinary Day   ◆ Unlucky Day

Lucky Hours	Direction of Happiness	Direction of Wealth	Direction of Opportunity
01-03 03-05 11-13 13-15 15-17 17-19	NW	E	SW
03-05 05-07 09-11 11-13 15-17	SW	E	S
23-01 01-03 05-07 07-09 09-11 13-15 17-19	S	S	E
23-01 01-03 03-05 07-09 09-11 15-17	SE	S	SE
01-03 03-05 05-07 09-11 13-15	NE	SE	NE
23-01 01-03 03-05 05-07 13-15	NW	SE	SW
23-01 01-03 09-11 17-19 19-21	SW	W	W

Snake – You must have the guts to face the difficulties ahead. *Horse* – Every cloud has a silver lining. *Ox* – Don't make any important changes at work this week. *Tiger* – Make sure that the windows and doors of your house are securely locked. *Mouse* – There will be rumour and gossip about your romance. *Pig* – Try to take good care of yourself, or you will suffer from different infections.

Date	Day	Favourable Activities
May 14	Mon	★ Engagement, Grand Opening, Animal Acquiring, Travelling, Trading, Signing Contracts, Construction
15	Tue	• Capturing, Fishing
16	Wed	• Worship, Start Learning, Travelling, Social Gathering
17	Thu	★ Worship, Trading, Signing Contracts, Travelling, Construction, Burial
18	Fri	★ Blessing, Moving, Tailoring, Animal Acquiring, Engagement, Wedding
19	Sat	★ Worship, Blessing, House Cleaning, Travelling, Construction, Hair Cutting, Grand Opening, Burial
20	Sun	• Worship

★ Lucky Day   • Ordinary Day   ◆ Unlucky Day

Lucky Hours	Direction of Happiness	Direction of Wealth	Direction of Opportunity
23-01 09-11 11-13 17-19	S	W	NW
01-03 05-07 07-09 09-11 11-13 13-15	SE	N	NE
23-01 03-05 05-07 11-13 13-15	NE	N	SW
01-03 03-05 07-09 09-11 11-13 13-15	NW	E	NE
01-03 03-05 09-11 11-13 13-15 19-21	SW	E	NE
01-03 03-05 05-07 09-11 13-15	S	S	E
23-01 03-05 05-07 09-11 11-13 19-21	SE	S	E

Rabbit – You must try to avoid a serious quarrel with your loved ones or you will be very sorry. *Dragon* – You will be most successful through negotiations and bargaining. *Sheep* – Although you will be very busy with social gatherings, loneliness will follow you like a shadow. *Monkey* – It's a good time to carry out new projects, or to start a new business. *Rooster* – Don't go swimming or fishing alone.

Date	Day	Favourable Activities
May 21	Mon	• Worship, House Cleaning, Bathing, Passage Fixing
22	Tue	★ Travelling, Wedding, Grand Opening, Construction, Signing Contracts, Trading, Moving, Burial
23	Wed	• Worship, Social Gathering, Hair Cutting, Capturing
24	Thu	◆ Unlucky Day Not suitable for important activities
25	Fri	• Social Gathering, Bathing, Tailoring, Stove Set-up
26	Sat	★ Start Learning, Travelling, Trading, Planting, Grand Opening, Engagement, Animal Acquiring, Burial
27	Sun	★ Wedding, Animal Acquiring, Signing Contracts, Engagement, Moving, Travelling, Trading, Burial

★ Lucky Day   • Ordinary Day   ◆ Unlucky Day

Lucky Hours			Direction of Happiness	Direction of Wealth	Direction of Opportunity
23-01	01-03	07-09	NE	SE	SW
09-11	13-15	15-17			
17-19					
23-01	01-03	03-05	NW	SE	SW
07-09	15-17	17-19			
23-01	03-05	05-07	SW	W	W
09-11	15-17	17-19			
19-21					
01-03	03-05	11-13	S	W	W
13-15	17-19	19-21			
01-03	05-07	07-09	SE	N	NE
09-11	15-17	17-19			
23-01	03-05	05-07	NE	N	N
09-11	15-17	17-19			
01-03	03-05	05-07	NW	E	NE
07-09					

Pig – Watch out, you must stop any illegal activities at once. *Dog* – You will be quite fortunate in money affairs, but should not be too greedy. *Tiger* – Calm down, and try to release yourself from the burden of a heavy workload. *Rabbit* – Hope for the best and prepare for the worst. *Mouse* – Your health is improving day by day. *Monkey* – You should try to improve business relationships with your clients.

Date	Day	Favourable Activities
May 28	Mon	★ Worship, Grand Opening, Start Learning, Travelling, Trading, Planting, Wedding, Construction
29	Tue	• Net Weaving, Hunting
30	Wed	• Social Gathering, Tailoring
31	Thu	★ Blessing, House Cleaning, Travelling, Moving, Engagement, Wedding, Animal Acquiring, Burial
Jun 1	Fri	• Worship, House Cleaning
2	Sat	★ Wedding, Grand Opening, Travelling, Moving, Engagement, Signing Contracts, Construction, Door Fixing
3	Sun	★ Grand Opening, Construction, Trading, Moving, Travelling, Wedding, Signing Contracts, Burial

★ Lucky Day   • Ordinary Day   ◆ Unlucky Day

Lucky Hours	Direction of Happiness	Direction of Wealth	Direction of Opportunity
03-05 05-07 09-11 11-13 19-21	SW	E	NE
01-03 03-05 05-07 09-11 17-19	S	S	E
23-01 05-07 07-09 09-11 15-17 19-21	SE	S	SE
01-03 03-05 13-15 17-19	NE	SE	SW
23-01 03-05 05-07 15-17 19-21	NW	SE	SW
23-01 01-03 09-11 13-15 15-17 17-19 19-21	SW	W	W
01-03 11-13 13-15 17-19	S	W	NW

Ox – It's time for you to take action in your career now. *Snake* – You can't afford to be late for any of your business meetings within this period. *Dragon* – You will hear good news from overseas. *Horse* – Don't be too picky when dealing with your lover and friends, or you will be very sorry. *Rooster* – You will have some luck with lotteries and gambling. *Sheep* – You must firmly reject the temptation of drugs this week.

Date	Day	Favourable Activities
Jun 4	Mon	★ Blessing, Hair Cutting, Wedding, Moving, Construction, Planting
5	Tue	◆ Unlucky Day Not suitable for important activities
6	Wed	◆ Unlucky Day Not suitable for important activities
7	Thu	● Worship, Social Gathering, Crack Refilling
8	Fri	★ Construction, Trading, Grand Opening, Planting, Wedding, Money Collecting, Travelling, Net Weaving
9	Sat	● Worship, Net Weaving
10	Sun	◆ Worship, Blessing, Start Learning, Travelling

★ Lucky Day   ● Ordinary Day   ◆ Unlucky Day

Lucky Hours			Direction of Happiness	Direction of Wealth	Direction of Opportunity
01-03 05-07 11-13 13-15 15-17			SE	N	NE
23-01 03-05 05-07 11-13 13-15 15-17			NE	N	SW
01-03 13-15 15-17 17-19			NW	E	NE
01-03 03-05 05-07 09-11 11-13 15-17			SW	E	NE
01-03 03-05 05-07 13-15 19-21			S	S	E
03-05 05-07 19-21			SE	S	E
01-03 03-05 07-09 13-15 17-19			NE	SE	SW

Rabbit – You should never criticize your colleagues or superiors during this period. *Mouse* – If you play with fire, you will get burned. *Dragon* – You should try to be humble enough to accept different ideas if you want to get out of trouble. *Pig* – It's time for you to travel; you will come back much refreshed. *Sheep* – Knowledge is power. Snake – Be patient or things will get out of control.

Date	Day	Favourable Activities
Jun 11	Mon	◆ Unlucky Day Not suitable for important activities
12	Tue	• Worship
13	Wed	★ Grand Opening, Wedding, Door Fixing, Construction, Travelling, Moving, Tailoring, Money Collecting
14	Thu	★ Blessing, Tailoring, Travelling, Grand Opening, Moving, Wedding, Construction, Crack Refilling
15	Fri	★ Worship, Bathing, Hair Cutting, House Cleaning, Wall Decorating, Passage Fixing
16	Sat	★ Blessing, Trading, Travelling, Signing Contracts, Grand Opening, Engagement, Wedding, Construction
17	Sun	◆ Unlucky Day Not suitable for important activities

★ Lucky Day   • Ordinary Day   ◆ Unlucky Day

Lucky Hours			Direction of Happiness	Direction of Wealth	Direction of Opportunity
01-03 15-17 17-19 19-21			NW	SE	N
09-11 11-13 15-17 17-19 19-21			SW	W	NW
09-11 11-13 13-15 17-19			S	W	NW
01-03 07-09 09-11 13-15 15-17			SE	N	SW
07-09 09-11 11-13 13-15 15-17			NE	N	SW
01-03 11-13 13-15 15-17			NW	E	SW
01-03 03-05 05-07 11-13 13-15 19-21			SW	E	S

Tiger – It's time for you to reveal your outstanding leadership qualities. *Horse* – If you can't beat them, join them. *Monkey* – You had better pay all your bills as soon as possible. *Dog* – Don't be shy about expressing your affection and true feeling this week. *Ox* – This will be a profitable week for you. *Rooster* – You must take good care of your eyes and ears, and go to see a doctor if anything seems amiss.

Date	Day	Favourable Activities
Jun 18	Mon	◆ Unlucky Day Not suitable for important activities
19	Tue	• Worship
20	Wed	◆ Unlucky Day Not suitable for important activities
21	Thu	◆ Unlucky Day (Solar Eclipse) Not suitable for important activities
22	Fri	★ Travelling, Wedding, Construction, Moving, Bed Set-up, Nursery Set-up, Engagement
23	Sat	• Crack Refilling, Tailoring
24	Sun	• Worship

★ Lucky Day   • Ordinary Day   ◆ Unlucky Day

Lucky Hours			Direction of Happiness	Direction of Wealth	Direction of Opportunity
01-03 03-05 05-07 07-09 09-11 13-15			S	S	E
01-03 07-09 09-11 15-17 17-19 19-21			SE	S	E
03-05 07-09 13-15 17-19 19-21			NE	SE	NE
03-05 05-07 13-15 15-17 19-21			NW	SE	SW
09-11 15-17 17-19			SW	W	W
01-03 09-11 11-13 13-15 17-19 19-21			S	W	W
05-07 09-11 13-15 15-17 17-19			SE	N	SW

Snake – You must not provoke your loved ones during this period. *Ox* – Too many cooks spoil the broth. *Rooster* – Don't be too ambitious or aggressive in business or in your personal life. *Horse* – You will have extra income this week. *Sheep* – You have to take good care of the health of elder family members at home. *Tiger* – You will have enough energy and intelligence to beat your opponents now.

Date	Day	Favourable Activities
Jun 25	Mon	★ Signing Contracts, Planting, House Cleaning, Construction, Travelling, Trading, Moving
26	Tue	★ Blessing, Travelling, Tailoring, Construction, Hair Cutting, Moving, Grand Opening, Burial
27	Wed	• Wall Decorating, Passage Fixing, House Cleaning, Hair Cutting
28	Thu	★ Blessing, Signing Contracts, Trading, Wedding, Tailoring
29	Fri	◆ Unlucky Day Not suitable for important activities
30	Sat	◆ Unlucky Day Not suitable for important activities
Jul 1	Sun	• Worship, Hair Cutting

★ Lucky Day   • Ordinary Day   ◆ Unlucky Day

Lucky Hours	Direction of Happiness	Direction of Wealth	Direction of Opportunity
03-05 05-07 09-11 11-13 13-15 15-17	NE	N	SW
01-03 07-09 09-11 11-13 13-15 15-17	NW	E	SW
03-05 07-09 09-11 11-13	SW	E	NE
03-05 05-07 09-11 13-15 19-21	S	S	E
03-05 05-07 07-09 11-13 19-21	SE	S	E
01-03 03-05 07-09 13-15 15-17	NE	SE	NE
01-03 03-05 05-07 15-17 17-19	NW	SE	N

Dragon – Don't risk your money, because your fortune is going up and down like a roller-coaster this week. *Rabbit* – You should watch your safety in water very carefully during this period. *Mouse* – Stop your dirty tricks, because they simply won't work. *Dog* – Your strong determination will scare away your opponents. *Monkey* – Waste not, want not. *Pig* – You will meet an attractive new person this week.

Date	Day	Favourable Activities
Jul 2	Mon	★ Grand Opening, Construction, Travelling, Trading, Wedding, Start Learning, Engagement, Burial
3	Tue	• Worship
4	Wed	★ Start Learning, Moving, Social Gathering, Tailoring, Construction, Nursery Set-up, Planting, Engagement
5	Thu	◆ Unlucky Day (Lunar Eclipse) Not suitable for important activities
6	Fri	• Wall Decorating
7	Sat	★ Blessing, Engagement, Travelling, Moving, Tailoring, Wedding
8	Sun	• Worship, Blessing, Bathing, House Cleaning

★ Lucky Day   • Ordinary Day   ◆ Unlucky Day

Lucky Hours			Direction of Happiness	Direction of Wealth	Direction of Opportunity
05-07	11-13	17-19	SW	W	W
03-05	11-13	13-15	S	W	NW
01-03 05-07 09-11 13-15 15-17 17-19			SE	N	NE
03-05 11-13 13-15 15-17			NE	N	SW
01-03 03-05 11-13 13-15 15-17 17-19			NW	E	SW
03-05 05-07 09-11 11-13 15-17			SW	E	S
23-01 05-07 07-09 09-11 13-15 17-19			S	S	E

Rooster – You must not cheat on your lover this week, or you will be very sorry. *Tiger* – Stand up firm against your opponents, or you will be beaten. *Horse* – Watch out for fire at home. *Mouse* – You should reject any invitations for new joint ventures, or there will be endless trouble later on. *Dog* – Don't go too near the edge of cliffs or other high places to avoid a sudden big fall.

Date	Day	Favourable Activities
Jul 9	Mon	• Worship, Bathing, House Cleaning
10	Tue	• Worship, Wall Decorating
11	Wed	◆ Unlucky Day Not suitable for important activities
12	Thu	• Bathing, Hair Cutting, Capturing
13	Fri	◆ Unlucky Day Not suitable for important activities
14	Sat	★ Engagement, Bed Set-up, Travelling, Trading, Grand Opening, Signing Contracts, Tailoring
15	Sun	★ Worship, Grand Opening, Animal Acquiring, Planting, Moving, Wedding, Travelling, Construction

★ Lucky Day   • Ordinary Day   ◆ Unlucky Day

Lucky Hours	Direction of Happiness	Direction of Wealth	Direction of Opportunity
23-01 03-05 07-09 09-11 15-17	SE	S	SE
03-05 05-07 09-11 13-15	NE	SE	NE
23-01 03-05 05-07 13-15	NW	SE	SW
23-01 09-11 17-19 19-21	SW	W	W
23-01 09-11 11-13 17-19	S	W	NW
05-07 07-09 09-11 11-13 13-15	SE	N	NE
23-01 03-05 05-07 11-13 13-15	NE	N	SW

Monkey – Mind your tongue at social gatherings this week. *Ox* – Don't risk your money in gambling or investments. *Sheep* – Watch out, big fish eat little fish. *Pig* – If the shoe fits, wear it. *Snake* – Keep on going, because your fortune is changing for the better. *Dragon* – Keep away from false friends. *Rabbit* – Keep your eyes open to avoid money and business traps.

Date	Day	Favourable Activities
Jul 16	Mon	• Worship, Money Collecting, Planting, Capturing
17	Tue	• Worship, Start Learning
18	Wed	• Net Weaving, Burial
19	Thu	• Worship, Travelling, Social Gathering, Wedding
20	Fri	★ Engagement, Wedding, Moving, Construction, Grand Opening, Travelling, Hair Cutting, Burial
21	Sat	• Worship, House Cleaning, Bathing, Burial
22	Sun	• Worship, Hunting, Net Weaving, Fishing

★ Lucky Day   • Ordinary Day   ◆ Unlucky Day

Lucky Hours	Direction of Happiness	Direction of Wealth	Direction of Opportunity
03-05 07-09 09-11 11-13 13-15	NW	E	NE
03-05 09-11 11-13 13-15 19-21	SW	E	NE
03-05 05-07 09-11 13-15	S	S	E
23-01 03-05 05-07 09-11 11-13 19-21	SE	S	E
23-01 07-09 09-11 13-15 15-17 17-19	NE	SE	SW
23-01 03-05 07-09 15-17 17-19	NW	SE	SW
23-01 03-05 05-07 09-11 15-17 17-19 19-21	SW	W	W

Snake – You will be very successful if you have determination and confidence. *Monkey* – Don't show off too much or you may suffer a robbery or break-in. *Tiger* – You will have to work harder this week because there are not any short-cuts. *Dragon* – You have to watch your budget closely to avoid financial problems. *Rooster* – Silence is golden. *Mouse* – Don't forget your medical appointments.

Date	Day	Favourable Activities
Jul 23	Mon	◆ Unlucky Day Not suitable for important activities
24	Tue	● Bathing, Hair Cutting, Tailoring, Capturing
25	Wed	◆ Unlucky Day Not suitable for important activities
26	Thu	★ Social Gathering, Signing Contracts, Trading, Engagement, Bed Set-up, Planting, Grand Opening, Burial
27	Fri	★ Start Learning, Grand Opening, Construction, Moving, Trading, Signing Contracts, Wedding, Travelling
28	Sat	● Worship, Capturing, Planting, Animal Acquiring
29	Sun	● Worship, Door Fixing, Social Gathering, Start Learning

★ Lucky Day   ● Ordinary Day   ◆ Unlucky Day

Lucky Hours			Direction of Happiness	Direction of Wealth	Direction of Opportunity
03-05	11-13	13-15	S	W	W
17-19	19-21				
05-07	07-09	09-11	SE	N	NE
15-17	17-19				
23-01	03-05	05-07	NE	N	N
09-11	15-17	17-19			
03-05	05-07	07-09	NW	E	NE
03-05	05-07	09-11	SW	E	NE
11-13	19-21				
03-05	05-07	09-11	S	S	E
17-19					
23-01	05-07	07-09	SE	S	SE
09-11	15-17	19-21			

Horse – Although you are quite fortunate this week, you should try to save more money for the future. *Rabbit* – You have to drive with extreme care this week. *Ox* – Of two evils, choose the lesser. *Dog* – Don't play with fire in your love affairs. *Sheep* – Watch out for the cleanliness of your food to avoid food poisoning. *Pig* – Don't jump up to a conclusion at this stage; reconsider the whole situation.

Date	Day	Favourable Activities
Jul 30	Mon	★ Worship, Crack Refilling, Tailoring, Burial
31	Tue	★ Worship, Animal Acquiring, Wedding, Bed Set-up, Travelling, Engagement
Aug 1	Wed	★ Worship, Door Fixing, Construction, House Cleaning, Hair Cutting, Planting
2	Thu	★ Blessing, Animal Acquiring, Bed Set-up, Door Fixing, Burial
3	Fri	• Worship, Net Weaving
4	Sat	◆ Unlucky Day Not suitable for important activities
5	Sun	• Worship, Bathing, Hair Cutting, Start Learning

★ Lucky Day   • Ordinary Day   ◆ Unlucky Day

Lucky Hours	Direction of Happiness	Direction of Wealth	Direction of Opportunity
03-05 13-15 17-19	NE	SE	SW
23-01 03-05 05-07 15-17 19-21	NW	SE	SW
23-01 09-11 13-15 15-17 17-19 19-21	SW	W	W
11-13 13-15 17-19	S	W	NW
05-07 11-13 13-15 15-17	SE	N	NE
23-01 03-05 05-07 11-13 13-15 15-17	NE	N	SW
13-15 15-17 17-19	NW	E	NE

Rooster – You had better take the necessary injections before any journey. *Ox* – God helps those who help themselves. *Monkey* – Keep alert; don't be blinded by your temporary success. *Pig* – Watch out for sharp knives and broken glass. *Snake* – It's time to improve your relationship with your lover. *Tiger* – You will be very productive at work if you can concentrate on your prime objective.

Date	Day	Favourable Activities
Aug 6	Mon	◆ Unlucky Day Not suitable for important activities
7	Tue	★ Engagement, Grand Opening, Social Gathering, Trading, Animal Acquiring, Signing Contracts, Bed Set-up, Burial
8	Wed	★ Blessing, Bed Set-up, Signing Contracts, Travelling, Moving, Wedding, Trading, Burial
9	Thu	● Worship, Start Learning
10	Fri	◆ Unlucky Day Not suitable for important activities
11	Sat	★ Worship, Construction, Ditching, Bed Set-up, Start Learning, Travelling
12	Sun	● Worship, Start Learning

★ Lucky Day   ● Ordinary Day   ◆ Unlucky Day

Lucky Hours	Direction of Happiness	Direction of Wealth	Direction of Opportunity
03-05 05-07 09-11 11-13 15-17	SW	E	NE
03-05 05-07 13-15 19-21	S	S	E
23-01 05-07 19-21	SE	S	E
23-01 01-03 07-09 13-15 17-19	NE	SE	SW
23-01 01-03 15-17 17-19 19-21	NW	SE	N
09-11 11-13 15-17 17-19 19-21	SW	W	NW
09-11 11-13 13-15 17-19	S	W	NW

Dog – You have to cut down on your extravagant tastes and habits. *Horse* – Don't gamble your money because your fortune is at a low ebb. *Sheep* – Some old friends will come to see you from overseas at the weekend. *Mouse* – Follow your doctor's instructions or you will be sorry. *Rabbit* – There are no great losses without some gain. *Dragon* – One bad apple spoils the whole barrel.

Date	Day	Favourable Activities
Aug 13	Mon	★ Blessing, Wedding, Travelling, Hair Cutting, Moving, Burial
14	Tue	• Hair Cutting, House Cleaning, Bathing, Burial
15	Wed	• Crack Refilling, Animal Acquiring, Planting
16	Thu	◆ Unlucky Day Not suitable for important activities
17	Fri	★ Construction, Travelling, Trading, Wedding, Grand Opening, Moving, Signing Contracts, Burial
18	Sat	★ Blessing, Planting, Capturing, Travelling, Construction, Animal Acquiring, Burial
19	Sun	◆ Unlucky Day Not suitable for important activities

★ Lucky Day　　• Ordinary Day　　◆ Unlucky Day

Lucky Hours	Direction of Happiness	Direction of Wealth	Direction of Opportunity
01-03 07-09 09-11 13-15 15-17	SE	N	SW
23-01 07-09 09-11 11-13 13-15 15-17	NE	N	SW
01-03 11-13 13-15 15-17	NW	E	SW
01-03 05-07 11-13 13-15 19-21	SW	E	S
23-01 01-03 05-07 07-09 09-11 13-15	S	S	E
23-01 01-03 07-09 09-11 15-17 17-19 19-21	SE	S	E
07-09 13-15 17-19 19-21	NE	SE	NE

Tiger – Don't walk alone in the quiet streets at night this week.
Mouse – Your health will be much improved within this period.
Rooster – Don't hesitate, because opportunity doesn't knock twice.
Monkey – Better to wear out than to rust away. *Rabbit* – You should carry out your work step by step to avoid a sudden big fall. *Ox* – Don't lend money because it will be difficult to get it back later.

Date	Day	Favourable Activities
Aug 20	Mon	• Worship, Burial
21	Tue	• Worship, Start Learning, Engagement
22	Wed	★ Grand Opening, Engagement, Wedding, Moving, Signing Contracts, Trading
23	Thu	★ Blessing, Start Learning, Engagement, Wedding, Moving, Grand Opening, Construction, Ditching
24	Fri	• Construction, Crack Refilling
25	Sat	★ Travelling, Door Fixing, House Cleaning, Bathing, Animal Acquiring, Money Collecting
26	Sun	• House Cleaning, Bathing, Hair Cutting, Burial

★ Lucky Day   • Ordinary Day   ◆ Unlucky Day

Lucky Hours	Direction of Happiness	Direction of Wealth	Direction of Opportunity
05-07 13-15 15-17 19-21	NW	SE	SW
09-11 15-17 17-19	SW	W	W
01-03 09-11 11-13 13-15 17-19 19-21	S	W	W
05-07 09-11 13-15 15-17 17-19	SE	N	SW
05-07 09-11 11-13 13-15 15-17	NE	N	SW
01-03 07-09 09-11 11-13 13-15 15-17	NW	E	SW
07-09 09-11 11-13	SW	E	NE

Snake – Your bargaining power is quite strong this week, so you should try to make good use of it. *Pig* – No pain, no gain. *Dragon* – Watch out, you will easily be fooled by appearances during this period. *Sheep* – When in Rome, do as the Romans do. *Dog* – You should double-check your accounting systems to make sure there aren't any flaws. *Horse* – Wake up, stop indulging in sex and alcohol.

Date	Day	Favourable Activities
Aug 27	Mon	★ Wedding, Planting, Construction, Moving, Animal Acquiring, Grand Opening, Net Weaving, Burial
28	Tue	◆ Unlucky Day Not suitable for important activities
29	Wed	★ Worship, Signing Contracts, Wedding, Moving, Construction, Travelling, Grand Opening, Money Collecting
30	Thu	• Animal Acquiring, Capturing
31	Fri	◆ Unlucky Day Not suitable for important activities
Sep 1	Sat	★ Grand Opening, Wedding, Bed Set-up, Trading, Engagement, Signing Contracts, Travelling, Burial
3	Sun	★ Start Learning, Social Gathering, Trading, Grand Opening, Animal Acquiring, Construction, Burial

★ Lucky Day   • Ordinary Day   ◆ Unlucky Day

Lucky Hours	Direction of Happiness	Direction of Wealth	Direction of Opportunity
05-07 09-11 13-15 19-21	S	S	E
05-07 07-09 11-13 19-21	SE	S	E
23-01 01-03 07-09 13-15 15-17	NE	SE	NE
23-01 01-03 05-07 15-17 17-19	NW	SE	N
23-01 05-07 11-13 17-19	SW	W	W
11-13 13-15	S	W	NW
01-03 05-07 09-11 13-15 15-17 17-19	SE	N	NE

Monkey – You must try to get enough rest and sleep in order to avoid a sudden physical collapse. *Mouse* – You should keep your eyes open if you are looking for a new romance. *Dog* – If you want something done well, do it yourself. *Ox* – This is no time to go off on any adventures. *Horse* – Old habits die hard. *Tiger* – A very heavy work schedule awaits you this week.

Date	Day	Favourable Activities
Sep 3	Mon	★ Moving, Animal Acquiring, Signing Contracts, Construction, Planting, Wedding, Grand Opening
4	Tue	• Worship, Start Learning, Construction, Ditching
5	Wed	• Worship, Construction, Wall Decorating, Travelling
6	Thu	★ Engagement, Stove Set-up, Moving, Wedding, Social Gathering, Travelling, Grand Opening, Burial
7	Fri	★ House Cleaning, Hair Cutting, Animal Acquiring, Construction, Burial
8	Sat	• Travelling, Planting, Hair Cutting, House Cleaning
9	Sun	◆ Unlucky Day Not suitable for important activities

★ Lucky Day   • Ordinary Day   ◆ Unlucky Day

Lucky Hours	Direction of Happiness	Direction of Wealth	Direction of Opportunity
23-01 11-13 13-15 15-17	NE	N	SW
01-03 11-13 13-15 15-17 17-19	NW	E	SW
05-07 09-11 11-13 15-17	SW	E	S
23-01 01-03 05-07 07-09 09-11 13-15 17-19	S	S	E
23-01 01-03 07-09 09-11 15-17	SE	S	SE
01-03 03-05 09-11 13-15	NE	SE	NE
23-01 01-03 03-05 13-15	NW	SE	SW

Rabbit – Watch your hard-earned rewards, or they will be swallowed up by somebody else. *Pig* – Never challenge superiors during this period. *Sheep* – Stop playing dirty tricks because they fool no one. *Dragon* – You will be able to choose investments wisely. *Snake* – Actions are more precious than words. *Rooster* – Keep away from raw or strange foods when travelling.

Date	Day	Favourable Activities
Sep 10	Mon	• Worship, Bathing, Passage Fixing, Wall Decorating
11	Tue	★ Trading, Grand Opening, Signing Contracts, Construction, Wedding
12	Wed	• Capturing, Hair Cutting, Bathing, Stove Set-up
13	Thu	◆ Unlucky Day Not suitable for important activities
14	Fri	★ Blessing, Moving, Wedding, Grand Opening, Travelling, Trading, Bed Set-up, Burial
15	Sat	★ Worship, Construction, Start Learning, Trading, Wedding, Grand Opening, Engagement, Moving
16	Sun	• Worship, Capturing

★ Lucky Day   • Ordinary Day   ◆ Unlucky Day

Lucky Hours			Direction of Happiness	Direction of Wealth	Direction of Opportunity
23-01 01-03 09-11 17-19 19-21			SW	W	W
23-01 09-11 11-13 17-19			S	W	NW
01-03 07-09 09-11 11-13 13-15			SE	N	NE
23-01 03-05 11-13 13-15			NE	N	SW
01-03 03-05 07-09 09-11 11-13 13-15			NW	E	NE
01-03 03-05 09-11 11-13 13-15 19-21			SW	E	NE
01-03 03-05 09-11 13-15			S	S	E

Ox – There will be a happy gathering of old mates this week. *Tiger* – Gambling will lead only to total destruction. *Snake* – A bird in the hand is worth two in the bush. *Monkey* – You have to put extra time and effort in at work if you want to survive. *Horse* – Say nothing about business secrets or your boss. *Rabbit* – It's the right time for vacation.

Date	Day	Favourable Activities
Sep 17	Mon	★ Blessing, Start Learning, Wedding, Travelling, Social Gathering, Engagement, Animal Acquiring
18	Tue	★ Planting, Hair Cutting, Tailoring, Burial
19	Wed	• Bathing, House Cleaning
20	Thu	• Travelling, Hair Cutting, House Cleaning, Planting
21	Fri	◆ Unlucky Day Not suitable for important activities
22	Sat	◆ Unlucky Day Not suitable for important activities
23	Sun	★ Engagement, Wedding, Social Gathering, Trading, Signing Contracts, Construction

★ Lucky Day   • Ordinary Day   ◆ Unlucky Day

Lucky Hours			Direction of Happiness	Direction of Wealth	Direction of Opportunity
23-01	03-05	09-11	SE	S	E
11-13	19-21				
23-01	01-03	07-09	NE	SE	SW
09-11	13-15	15-17			
17-19					
23-01	01-03	03-05	NW	SE	SW
07-09	15-17	17-19			
23-01	03-05	09-11	SW	W	W
15-17	17-19	19-21			
01-03	03-05	11-13	S	W	W
13-15	17-19	19-21			
01-03	07-09	09-11	SE	N	NE
15-17	17-19				
23-01	03-05	09-11	NE	N	N
15-17	17-19				

Sheep – Don't rely too much on others at work, you have to do your job all by yourself this week. *Rooster* – You will have luck in lottery and gambling. *Mouse* – Silence is golden. *Pig* – Work harder, there will be no short-cuts to your success. *Horse* – It's no use crying over spilled milk. *Rabbit* – Don't give up at this stage because your fortune will come good in the months to come.

Date	Day	Favourable Activities
Sep 24	Mon	• Hair Cutting, Bathing, Capturing, Burial
25	Tue	◆ Unlucky Day Not suitable for important activities
26	Wed	• Worship, Blessing, Tailoring
27	Thu	★ Start Learning, Moving, Construction, Grand Opening, Wedding, Social Gathering, Trading, Engagement
28	Fri	• Worship, Capturing
29	Sat	★ Grand Opening, Travelling, Tailoring, Moving, Money Collecting, Wedding, Start Learning, Social Gathering
30	Sun	★ Worship, Animal Acquiring, Hair Cutting, House Cleaning, Burial

★ Lucky Day   • Ordinary Day   ◆ Unlucky Day

Lucky Hours	Direction of Happiness	Direction of Wealth	Direction of Opportunity
01-03 03-05 07-09	NW	E	NE
03-05 09-11 11-13 19-21	SW	E	NE
01-03 03-05 09-11 17-19	S	S	E
23-01 07-09 09-11 15-17 19-21	SE	S	SE
01-03 03-05 13-15 17-19	NE	SE	SW
23-01 03-05 15-17 19-21	NW	SE	SW
23-01 01-03 09-11 13-15 15-17 17-19 19-21	SW	W	W

Dragon – You will be very successful if you make the right choice for your future. *Dog* – You tend to suffer from toothache, so try to keep your teeth and mouth clean. *Sheep* – Don't try your luck in money affairs this weekend, or you will be very sorry. *Mouse* – Try to make your work and ideas more organized. *Snake* – Don't indulge yourself too much in sex and pleasure, or you will miss out on opportunities.

Date	Day	Favourable Activities
Oct 1	Mon	• Worship, Bathing, House Cleaning
2	Tue	★ Worship, Construction, Planting, Travelling, House Cleaning, Hair Cutting
3	Wed	◆ Unlucky Day Not suitable for important activities
4	Thu	• Worship, Passage Fixing, Wall Decorating, Bathing
5	Fri	★ Social Gathering, Net Weaving, Door Fixing, Money Collecting, Tailoring
6	Sat	• Net Weaving, Capturing, Stove Set-up, Door Fixing
7	Sun	◆ Unlucky Day Not suitable for important activities

★ Lucky Day   • Ordinary Day   ◆ Unlucky Day

Lucky Hours	Direction of Happiness	Direction of Wealth	Direction of Opportunity
01-03 11-13 13-15 17-19	S	W	NW
01-03 11-13 13-15 15-17	SE	N	NE
23-01 03-05 11-13 13-15 15-17	NE	N	SW
01-03 13-15 15-17 17-19	NW	E	NE
01-03 03-05 09-11 11-13 15-17	SW	E	NE
01-03 03-05 13-15 19-21	S	S	E
23-01 03-05 19-21	SE	S	E

Pig – Mind your personal safety in the countryside. *Tiger* – You will have unexpected income this week. *Rooster* – The sooner begun, the sooner done. *Horse* – Stop your weeping, let bygones be bygones. *Rabbit* – Cheer up, God helps those who help themselves. *Monkey* – Never try to betray your colleagues or superiors or there will be endless trouble later on. *Ox* – You must take good care of your wallet in crowded places.

Date	Day	Favourable Activities
Oct 8	Mon	• Worship, Bed Set-up, Capturing, Hunting
9	Tue	◆ Unlucky Day Not suitable for important activities
10	Wed	★ Construction, Wedding, Grand Opening, Moving, Trading, Signing Contracts, Start Learning, Burial
11	Thu	• Capturing, Hunting
12	Fri	★ Engagement, Start Learning, Moving, Travelling, Grand Opening, Ditching, Construction, Wedding
13	Sat	• Crack Refilling, Hair Cutting, House Cleaning
14	Sun	★ Worship, Travelling, Tailoring, Moving, Animal Acquiring, Money Collecting

★ Lucky Day   • Ordinary Day   ◆ Unlucky Day

Lucky Hours			Direction of Happiness	Direction of Wealth	Direction of Opportunity
23-01 01-03 03-05 07-09 13-15 17-19			NE	SE	SW
23-01 01-03 15-17 17-19 19-21			NW	SE	N
09-11 11-13 15-17 17-19 19-21			SW	W	NW
09-11 11-13 13-15 17-19			S	W	NW
01-03 09-11 13-15 15-17			SE	N	SW
23-01 09-11 11-13 13-15 15-17			NE	N	SW
01-03 11-13 13-15 15-17			NW	E	SW

Snake – It's definitely not a good time to make any investments, or you will be the big loser. *Rabbit* – You will be quite creative and productive this week, so try to make good use of this period. *Sheep* – Watch out, your fortune in money matters is on a downward trend. *Pig* – You will be quite passionate this week; you'd better try to control yourself. *Ox* – You should take good care of your children at home.

Date	Day	Favourable Activities
Oct 15	Mon	◆ Unlucky Day Not suitable for important activities
16	Tue	• Worship, Travelling, Bathing, Burial
17	Wed	• Passage Fixing
18	Thu	• Burial
19	Fri	• Worship, Bathing, Door Fixing, Bed Set-up
20	Sat	◆ Unlucky Day Not suitable for important activities
21	Sun	• Worship, Bed Set-up, Animal Acquiring, Hunting

★ Lucky Day   • Ordinary Day   ◆ Unlucky Day

Lucky Hours			Direction of Happiness	Direction of Wealth	Direction of Opportunity
01-03 03-05 05-07 11-13 13-15 19-21			SW	E	S
23-01 01-03 03-05 05-07 09-11 13-15			S	S	E
23-01 01-03 09-11 15-17 17-19 19-21			SE	S	E
03-05 13-15 17-19 19-21			NE	SE	NE
03-05 05-07 13-15 15-17 19-21			NW	SE	SW
09-11 15-17 17-19			SW	W	W
01-03 09-11 11-13 13-15 17-19 19-21			S	W	W

Mouse – Watch out, bad news travels fast. *Horse* – The harder you work, the luckier you get. *Dog* – Stop fooling around with money this week, or you will face endless trouble. *Dragon* – You must try to be punctual at business meetings or you will find yourself kicked out. *Tiger* – You should keep on upgrading yourself. *Rooster* – Strike while the iron is hot. *Monkey* – Don't play with fire in love affairs, or you will get burned.

Date	Day	Favourable Activities
Oct 22	Mon	★ Travelling, Engagement, Grand Opening, Trading, Construction, Moving, Wedding, Animal Acquiring
23	Tue	● Hunting, Capturing
24	Wed	★ Blessing, Nursery Set-up, Moving, Ditching, Start Learning, Grand Opening, Travelling
25	Thu	● Bathing, House Cleaning, Hair Cutting, Tailoring
26	Fri	★ Engagement, Social Gathering, Animal Acquiring, Travelling, Moving
27	Sat	◆ Unlucky Day Not suitable for important activities
28	Sun	● Worship, Start Learning, Bathing, Net Weaving

★ Lucky Day   ● Ordinary Day   ◆ Unlucky Day

Lucky Hours	Direction of Happiness	Direction of Wealth	Direction of Opportunity
05-07 09-11 13-15 15-17 17-19	SE	N	SW
03-05 05-07 09-11 11-13 13-15 15-17	NE	N	SW
01-03 09-11 11-13 13-15 15-17	NW	E	SW
03-05 09-11 11-13	SW	E	NE
03-05 05-07 09-11 13-15 19-21	S	S	E
03-05 05-07 11-13 19-21	SE	S	E
23-01 01-03 03-05 13-15 15-17	NE	SE	NE

Ox – Honesty is the best policy in personal and business affairs right now. *Pig* – It's the right time to buy property or valuables for yourself now. *Dragon* – You have to watch your health and safety very carefully this weekend. *Tiger* – Don't make a hasty decision in love this week. *Mouse* – You should never leave your children alone at home this week.

Date	Day	Favourable Activities
Oct 29	Mon	• Passage Fixing, Wall Decorating
30	Tue	• Construction, Burial
31	Wed	★ Worship, Wedding, Social Gathering, Construction, Burial
Nov 1	Thu	◆ Unlucky Day Not suitable for important activities
2	Fri	• Worship, Bed Set-up, Net Weaving, Hunting
3	Sat	★ Wedding, Grand Opening, Trading, Engagement, Moving, Construction, Travelling, Burial
4	Sun	• Worship, Capturing

★ Lucky Day   • Ordinary Day   ◆ Unlucky Day

Lucky Hours	Direction of Happiness	Direction of Wealth	Direction of Opportunity
23-01 01-03 03-05 05-07 15-17 17-19	NW	SE	N
23-01 05-07 11-13 17-19	SW	W	W
03-05 11-13 13-15	S	W	NW
01-03 05-07 09-11 13-15 15-17 17-19	SE	N	NE
23-01 03-05 11-13 13-15 15-17	NE	N	SW
01-03 03-05 11-13 13-15 15-17 17-19	NW	E	SW
03-05 05-07 09-11 11-13 15-17	SW	E	S

Snake – Many hands make light work, so don't hesitate to ask for help. *Sheep* – Don't exhaust yourself by burning the candle at both ends. *Rooster* – You may have the chance to meet your dream lover. *Horse* – You will hear good news from foreign countries this week. *Rabbit* – It's time to develop and maintain a close connection with your chief client. *Dog* – You must keep away from dangerous places while travelling.

Date	Day	Favourable Activities
Nov 5	Mon	★ Blessing, Start Learning, Construction, Grand Opening, Money Collecting, Planting, Moving, Travelling
6	Tue	★ Worship, Hair Cutting, Tailoring, House Cleaning, Wall Decorating
7	Wed	• Worship
8	Thu	◆ Unlucky Day Not suitable for important activities
9	Fri	★ Moving, Travelling, Bathing, Hair Cutting, Engagement, House Cleaning
10	Sat	• Worship
11	Sun	★ Wedding, Engagement, Money Collecting, Grand Opening, Trading, Burial

★ Lucky Day   • Ordinary Day   ◆ Unlucky Day

Lucky Hours	Direction of Happiness	Direction of Wealth	Direction of Opportunity
23-01 01-03 05-07 09-11 13-15 17-19	S	S	E
23-01 01-03 03-05 09-11 15-17	SE	S	E
01-03 03-05 05-07 09-11 13-15	NE	SE	NE
23-01 01-03 03-05 05-07 13-15	NW	SE	SW
23-01 01-03 17-19 19-21	SW	W	W
23-01 11-13 17-19	S	W	NW
01-03 05-07 07-09 11-13 13-15	SE	N	NE

Pig – You have to control your emotions and passions properly this week. *Rabbit* – Keep away from raw or spicy foods to avoid the risk of food poisoning. *Tiger* – You will be quite popular socially. *Sheep* – You have to be calm in the face of severe challenges and criticism during the week. *Dragon* – You may be able to meet someone attractive while travelling. *Horse* – Mind your own business, and don't be curious.

Date	Day	Favourable Activities
Nov 12	Mon	★ Blessing, Construction, Grand Opening, Wedding, Trading, Travelling, Moving, Burial
13	Tue	★ Worship, Wedding, Animal Acquiring, Moving, Hair Cutting, Engagement, Tailoring, Burial
14	Wed	◆ Unlucky Day Not suitable for important activities
15	Thu	● Worship, Tailoring, Hunting
16	Fri	★ Grand Opening, Engagement, Trading, Construction, Bed Set-up, Start Learning
17	Sat	★ Wedding, Start Learning, Travelling, Moving, Social Gathering, Planting, Construction, Burial
18	Sun	★ Construction, Hair Cutting, Tailoring, Animal Acquiring, Travelling, Wedding, Nursery Set-up, Start Learning

★ Lucky Day   ● Ordinary Day   ◆ Unlucky Day

Lucky Hours			Direction of Happiness	Direction of Wealth	Direction of Opportunity
23-01 03-05 05-07			NE	N	SW
11-13 13-15					
01-03 03-05 07-09			NW	E	NE
11-13 13-15					
01-03 03-05 11-13			SW	E	NE
13-15 19-21					
01-03 03-05 05-07			S	S	E
13-15					
23-01 03-05 05-07			SE	S	E
11-13 19-21					
23-01 01-03 07-09			NE	SE	SW
13-15 15-17 17-19					
23-01 01-03 03-05			NW	SE	SW
07-09 15-17 17-19					

Mouse – Laugh and the world laughs with you. *Monkey* – Watch out, there will be several unexpected expenses this week. *Rooster* – Never try to challenge or provoke your superiors this week. *Dog* – Stop fooling around, because your dirty tricks will never lead to prosperity right now. *Snake* – It never rains but it pours. *Ox* – You must try to pay all your bills as soon as possible.

Date	Day	Favourable Activities
Nov 19	Mon	• Tailoring, Net Weaving
20	Tue	◆ Unlucky Day Not suitable for important activities
21	Wed	• House Cleaning, Bathing, Construction, Start Learning
22	Thu	• Worship, Social Gathering, Crack Refilling
23	Fri	★ Moving, Wedding, Engagement, Grand Opening, Travelling, Trading, Burial
24	Sat	★ Grand Opening, Construction, Moving, Trading, Wedding, Engagement, Travelling, Grand Opening
25	Sun	• Net Weaving, Capturing, Hair Cutting, Hunting

★ Lucky Day   • Ordinary Day   ◆ Unlucky Day

Lucky Hours	Direction of Happiness	Direction of Wealth	Direction of Opportunity
23-01 03-05 05-07 15-17 17-19 19-21	SW	W	W
01-03 03-05 11-13 13-15 17-19 19-21	S	W	W
01-03 05-07 07-09 15-17 17-19	SE	N	NE
23-01 03-05 05-07 15-17 17-19	NE	N	N
01-03 03-05 05-07 07-09	NW	E	NE
03-05 05-07 11-13 19-21	SW	E	NE
01-03 03-05 05-07 17-19	S	S	E

Sheep – It is better to give than to receive. *Monkey* – You should walk and drive with extreme care during this week. *Pig* – Your relationship with your loved ones will be much improved within this period. *Dog* – Be money wise and watch out for money traps. *Snake* – No matter how busy you are, you should not forget about your sweet home. *Dragon* – You have to keep an optimistic and positive attitude at work for your survival.

Date	Day	Favourable Activities
Nov 26	Mon	◆ Unlucky Day Not suitable for important activities
27	Tue	★ Social Gathering, Engagement, Bed Set-up, Travelling, Moving, Construction, Wedding, Burial
28	Wed	★ Trading, Door Fixing, Construction, Signing Contracts, Grand Opening, Start Learning, Burial
29	Thu	● House Cleaning, Hunting, Capturing
30	Fri	★ Worship, Bed Set-up, House Cleaning, Start Learning, Construction
Dec 1	Sat	● Construction
2	Sun	◆ Unlucky Day Not suitable for important activities

★ Lucky Day   ● Ordinary Day   ◆ Unlucky Day

Lucky Hours			Direction of Happiness	Direction of Wealth	Direction of Opportunity
23-01 05-07 07-09 15-17 19-21			SE	S	SE
01-03 03-05 13-15 17-19			NE	SE	SW
23-01 03-05 05-07 15-17 19-21			NW	SE	SW
23-01 01-03 13-15 15-17 17-19 19-21			SW	W	W
01-03 11-13 13-15 17-19			S	W	NW
01-03 05-07 11-13 13-15 15-17			SE	N	NE
23-01 03-05 05-07 11-13 13-15 15-17			NE	N	SW

Ox – Don't forget about home safety, especially the safety of children at home this week. *Horse* – There are tricks to every trade, so don't be fooled by other people. *Mouse* – There will be an important breakthrough in your romance this week. *Tiger* – You will enjoy much greater achievements if you can concentrate on your prime target only. *Rooster* – Don't turn a cold shoulder to your friends and lover.

Date	Day	Favourable Activities
Dec 3	Mon	★ Travelling, House Cleaning, Wedding, Moving, Hair Cutting, Planting, Construction, Burial
4	Tue	• Social Gathering, Hair Cutting, Crack Refilling
5	Wed	★ Grand Opening, Moving, Construction, Trading, Planting, Wedding, Engagement, Travelling
6	Thu	★ Net Weaving, Wedding, Grand Opening, Moving, Money Collecting, Travelling, Engagement, Construction
7	Fri	★ Blessing, Travelling, Trading, Animal Acquiring, Engagement, Moving, Wedding, Construction
8	Sat	◆ Unlucky Day Not suitable for important activities
9	Sun	◆ Unlucky Day Not suitable for important activities

★ Lucky Day   • Ordinary Day   ◆ Unlucky Day

Lucky Hours			Direction of Happiness	Direction of Wealth	Direction of Opportunity
01-03	13-15	15-17	NW	E	NE
17-19					
01-03	03-05	05-07	SW	E	NE
11-13	15-17				
01-03	03-05	05-07	S	S	E
13-15	19-21				
23-01	03-05	05-07	SE	S	E
19-21					
23-01	01-03	03-05	NE	SE	SW
07-09	13-15	17-19			
23-01	01-03	15-17	NW	SE	N
17-19	19-21				
09-11	15-17	17-19	SW	W	NW
19-21					

Dog – You should not get mad, but try to get even when you face unfair treatment this week. *Dragon* – You are at the edge of exhaustion; get enough rest and sleep whenever possible. *Ox* – Out of debt, out of trouble. *Pig* – You will travel frequently within this period. *Sheep* – It's the right time to take a vacation. *Snake* – You'd better keep away from sharp knives and saws to avoid a serious injury.

Date	Day	Favourable Activities
Dec 10	Mon	• Worship
11	Tue	★ Start Learning, Grand Opening, Hair Cutting, Moving, Wedding, Travelling, Trading
12	Wed	• Bathing, Hair Cutting, House Cleaning, Hunting
13	Thu	★ Blessing, Nursery Set-up, Planting, Start Learning, Construction, Ditching
14	Fri	◆ Unlucky Day Not suitable for important activities
15	Sat	• Worship, Wall Decorating
16	Sun	★ Wedding, Construction, Moving, Travelling, Grand Opening, Hair Cutting, Trading

★ Lucky Day   • Ordinary Day   ◆ Unlucky Day

Lucky Hours	Direction of Happiness	Direction of Wealth	Direction of Opportunity
09-11 13-15 17-19	S	W	NW
01-03 07-09 09-11 13-15 15-17	SE	N	SW
23-01 07-09 09-11 13-15 15-17	NE	N	SW
01-03 13-15 15-17	NW	E	SW
01-03 03-05 05-07 13-15 19-21	SW	E	S
23-01 01-03 03-05 05-07 07-09 09-11 13-15	S	S	E
23-01 01-03 07-09 09-11 15-17 17-19 19-21	SE	S	E

Rabbit – You must forget about any illegal activities, or you will be in deep trouble. Horse – You will be caught in a dilemma; it's better to ask for professional advice to solve the problem. Monkey – Do right and fear no man. Tiger – You should try to pay attention to your lover's complaints, or you will be very sorry. Mouse – You don't get something for nothing. Rooster – Silence is golden.

Date	Day	Favourable Activities
Dec 17	Mon	★ Travelling, Planting, Grand Opening, Trading, Construction, Net Weaving, Money Collecting, Signing Contracts
18	Tue	• Passage Fixing, Wall Decorating
19	Wed	★ Construction, Door Fixing, Trading, Engagement, Wedding, Net Weaving, Tailoring
20	Thu	• Worship, Capturing
21	Fri	◆ Unlucky Day Not suitable for important activities
22	Sat	• Hair Cutting, Fishing
23	Sun	★ Start Learning, Trading, Travelling, Moving, House Cleaning, Grand Opening, Burial

★ Lucky Day   • Ordinary Day   ◆ Unlucky Day

Lucky Hours	Direction of Happiness	Direction of Wealth	Direction of Opportunity
03-05 07-09 13-15 17-19 19-21	NE	SE	NE
03-05 05-07 13-15 15-17 19-21	NW	SE	SW
09-11 15-17 17-19	SW	W	W
01-03 09-11 13-15 17-19 19-21	S	W	W
05-07 09-11 13-15 15-17 17-19	SE	N	SW
03-05 05-07 09-11 13-15 15-17	NE	N	SW
01-03 07-09 09-11 13-15 15-17	NW	E	SW

Horse – You should try to spend more time with your lover and with family members this week. *Ox* – Your fortune in money affairs will be much improved this week. *Pig* – There's no great loss without some gain. *Mouse* – Don't expect too much from your love affairs, or you will be deeply disappointed. *Snake* – Don't be too greedy, half a loaf is better than none. *Tiger* – You should try not to get involved in any loans.

Date	Day	Favourable Activities
Dec 24	Mon	• Hair Cutting, Tailoring, Capturing, House Cleaning
25	Tue	★ Blessing, Engagement, Start Learning, Grand Opening, Nursery Set-up, Construction
26	Wed	◆ Unlucky Day Not suitable for important activities
27	Thu	• Bathing, Hair Cutting
28	Fri	★ Blessing, Travelling, Wedding, Social Gathering, Trading, Moving, Construction, Burial
29	Sat	★ Social Gathering, Planting, Tailoring, Travelling, Moving, Signing Contracts, Grand Opening, Trading
30	Sun	• Wall Decorating, Passage Fixing
31	Mon	★ Blessing, Wedding, Construction, Signing Contracts, Engagements, Trading, Animal Acquiring

★ Lucky Day   • Ordinary Day   ◆ Unlucky Day

Lucky Hours	Direction of Happiness	Direction of Wealth	Direction of Opportunity
03-05 07-09 09-11	SW	E	NE
03-05 05-07 09-11 13-15 19-21	S	S	E
03-05 05-07 07-09 19-21	SE	S	E
23-01 01-03 03-05 07-09 13-15 15-17	NE	SE	NE
23-01 01-03 03-05 05-07 15-17 17-19	NW	SE	N
23-01 05-07 17-19	SW	W	W
03-05 13-15	S	W	NW
01-03 05-07 09-11 13-15 15-17 17-19	SE	N	NE

Dragon – You are going to have a very romantic week. *Rooster* – Don't let your personal life get mixed up with your business. *Monkey* – Be more considerate, or you will be somewhat isolated by the people round you. *Rabbit* – It's not wise to try your luck at gambling or investments during the week. *Sheep* – You should try to keep your promises, or you will be in deep trouble. *Dog* – There will be a breakthrough in your love affairs.